Merry 2010
Christmas, Henry.
I hope you enjoy
the book.
Your old room-
mate.
Another Henry.

Beckoning Horizons

by Henry Jay Enns

Beckoning Horizons

by Henry Jay Enns

ISBN 0-9682443-5-1

NEW LEAF WORKS
Edmonton, Alberta, Canada

Address all correspondence to:
Henry Jay Enns, Box 119, Rapid View, SK S0M 2M0
Fax (306) 236-2840
Email: henrye@powertochange.com

Dedicated to

Luella, Arlyn, Laurella, Lyndell, Lanna-Marie
and the Grandchildren

Photographs on pages 130 and 154 courtesy of Raymond L'Hirondelle. Photographs on pages 164 and 166 taken by Mildred Mallinger. Photograph on page 176 courtesy of Reid's Photo. Photographs on pages 160 and 189 courtesy of LaCrete & Area Chamber of Commerce.

Cover design by Elsie Montgomery

ACKNOWLEDGEMENTS

Someone has said ,"No man is an island". Certainly this statement is accurate in my story. To list the players in this game is impossible. There have been so many. They gave life, provided necessities, advised, taught, encouraged, worked, played, prayed, sold, bought, and not least of all, provided my reason for being. It is possible, however, to mention several to whom my debt is deepest and my gratitude fullest.

Although this is not to be an essentially religious book, I would be less than honest and most ungrateful if I did not acknowledge the Lord. He redeemed and rescued me, gave me direction, and established my goings. He gave wisdom and courage, provided and protected—and how he protected! It was his hand that tipped the balance in all of those, "What if...?" situations, any one of which could have precluded the writing of this account!

Secondly, and only secondly, I lift up "the wife of my youth!" Though one of the bravest people I know, her natural inclination is to live quietly. Certainly my most recent and current enthusiasm did not always coincide with her preferences, but she could understand that I was not designed to live in a box. Thus she did the things that good working wives do, and waited. She did the things that good mothers do and waited. She cooked the meals and waited to wash not only clothes and dishes but also that dirty, black, handle-less lunch bucket. Nor was her waiting of the normal kind; she did much of hers with the specter of widowhood looming in her imagination. Likely only the local undertaker has planned more funerals.

Then there are my children. They helped me live this book. How could I have been free to live as I did if not for their cooperation? Which father would not be inspired by the smile of a Laurella? Which father would not be proud of a Lanna-Marie. Which father would not profit by the help of a wise son like Arlyn and a skilled son like Lyndell? Even the writing of this book has been a joint effort. Luella has been very involved in advising, proof reading and editing. Several of her actual contributions are included. Lanna-Marie, using a very rough and confused hand written manuscript, typed the bulk of this book. Arlyn offered much information, proof read, and did most of the corrections to the original typed copy. Lyndell has patiently taken his old dad by the hand and guided him through the technical mysteries of this incredible lap-top.

Nor should I fail to mention my editor, Nathan Harms, who has put a large effort into the production of this book.

In all cases, I offer my deepest gratitude!

TABLE OF CONTENTS

FOREWORD

Recently I was asked to tell a group of youngsters a story. My account made reference to my fur trading days. After the meeting a young fellow about nine years old came to me and reported that he didn't believe my account. "You aren't old enough to have been a fur trader!" was his cynical verdict.

Soon I'll pass off the scene, and my stories with me, unless I record them. I prefer to have some of these accounts preserved for posterity. The nation of Israel's history was perpetuated with great accuracy. Why? So that future generations would look back and remember where they had come from. Having that knowledge they could then assert who they were, what they represented, and what they planned to be. Luella and I have often discussed this matter of book writing but we have been deterred by a concern about exposing and using people. On one occasion, my associate, Fleuri, and I were out horseback riding and checking the Co-op properties. In the course of our conversation I mentioned that I was reading a book written by a teacher who had taught in the community of a religious minority. Fleuri became very quiet and thoughtful. I could only guess at his thoughts. He might have been thinking, "So that's how these outsiders operate. They come into a community such as ours, learn how things are and then go off and write a book at our expense." I trust that no one will feel used for my having written this account.

As for the title of this book, I should like to explain that horizons are an interesting phenomenon in that, if you are at sea level your horizon is at eye level and if you rise to 10,000 feet, it is still at eye level. Similarly, life offers opportunities, challenges, dreams, goals, which lie out there to be achieved. As a person conquers the first one in his path there will be another, and then another. As the climber labours on and up there is always another objective to attain. And always the process is fuelled by hope.

Although I am a person of very modest talents, there has always been another horizon to be conquered and it has always been my concern that it be subdued. Life has been, and continues to be, an interesting experience. It is this writer's hope the reader will enjoy reliving a life that has been lived always on the threshold of another "Beckoning Horizon".

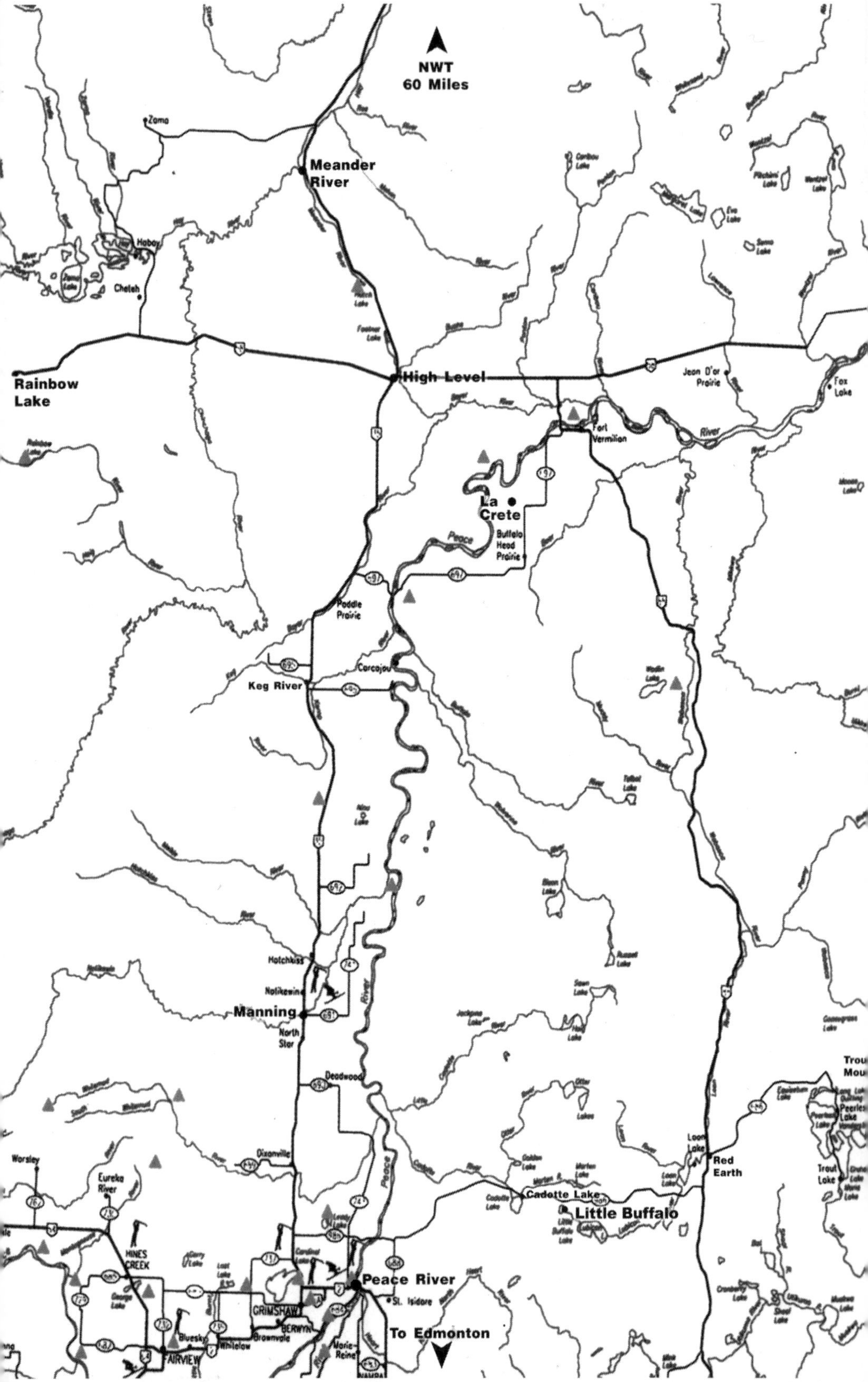

NWT
60 Miles
Zama
Meander River
Hay
Habay
Chateh
Rainbow Lake
High Level
Jean D'or Prairie
Fox Lake
Fort Vermilion
La Crete
Buffalo Head Prairie
Peace
River
Paddle Prairie
Carcajou
Keg River
Hotchkiss
Notikewin
Manning
North Star
Deadwood
Dixonville
Worsley
Eureka River
HINES CREEK
Cadotte Lake
Little Buffalo
Red Earth
Loon Lake
Trout Lake
Peerless Lake
Peace River
St. Isidore
GRIMSHAW
BERWYN
Brownvale
Bluesky
Whitelaw
AIRVIEW
Marie-Reine
To Edmonton

Chapter 1

Trout Mountain—It Can't Be!

Conversation in the cramped cabin of our little Cessna 140 came to a halt during the July, 1962 afternoon. The mood was sombre. Bob Stanton, my instructor, and I were fully preoccupied. The matter in which we were involved was a serious one, to be sure, nothing short of life and death. He tended to push left rudder while I preferred the right. Neither of us had the foggiest notion of direction, for the fog was all about us. Under normal circumstances, lakes along with maps offer reliable direction in navigation. But during this flight, even when we flew across a lake, it offered not a clue as to our position. From 200 feet in the air, one lake looks like a hundred others. So on we roared. Trees, muskegs and lakes swept under us, while seemingly innocent clouds taunted us from all sides as they witnessed our worsening predicament. Neither Bob nor I knew how this matter was going to be resolved but we knew that the answer to that question would be forthcoming within the next four hours. Our tanks would dry up in that time.

Our flight had been a dubious undertaking from the outset. We had hoped to leave Edmonton early that morning but we couldn't get clearance from the tower to depart until later. Even then conditions were well short of ideal. We were obliged to fly so low Bob was concerned we would terrorize the caged mink on the shores of Lesser Slave Lake. The weather lifted somewhat by the time we got to Peace River where we refuelled before setting off for Little Buffalo.

The purpose of our trip was twofold. I needed this cross-country trip with my instructor in order to get my license. Secondly, I wished to look in on my trading post which George and Delores Dunn were tending during the slack summer months.

Reaching Little Buffalo hadn't been difficult, but when we set off for Edmonton across the vast expanse of forest south of Little Buffalo, matters quickly deteriorated. We weren't long in concluding we were in serious trouble. What to do about our predicament was another matter. Turning back was not an option. To find Little Buffalo under our circumstances was a virtually impossibility. To the south there were at least some indications of human endeavour. But where were we to find one particular heading when any direction seemed as viable as the other three hundred fifty-nine points of the compass? Then suddenly, and one can only believe providentially, I saw a forestry tower out my left window.

In a part of the world where trails are a rarity and roads almost non-existent you can expect to find an airstrip near most fire-towers. Sure enough! A strip! True, it wasn't really an airstrip but there were a lot less trees on it than anywhere else! We didn't need a conference to decide our course of action.

Later the tower-man told us of his reaction. He was thoroughly deaf so when his son told him that he had heard a door slam, he had passed a scathing indictment on his son's intestinal condition. When the son heard the second door slam, Dad knew his son was crazy. We had landed on a strip used only by helicopters; but so be it. Standing on firm ground is a practice altogether too lightly esteemed by most. How we were to get out of there was not an immediate concern. We were alive; we were healthy; we were on terra firma!

As it happened, our host proved to be a real entertainer. He had a wealth of stories to tell, and he was quite prepared to share them with gusto typical of those who have long foregone human company. Saturday night passed, and with it, story time. Sunday we were back to the sombre realities of life.

The weather was in no hurry to clear, but by about noon the situation seemed to justify a try. Having borrowed a drum of Forestry gas (which I believe I paid for later), we fuelled the plane. We were ready to try our helicopter strip. On the north end of the strip there were several hundred feet of reasonably firm ground. This we used; but beyond that was a wet draw. When we hit that low spot, the mud grabbed at our wheels. They in their turn threw the mud into the prop; the prop threw it back at the windscreen. The resulting sound effects were not reassuring. By the time the mud had "cleared" we had lost our faltering momentum and any hope of flight was swamped. We tried several times but with the same nerve-wracking results every time. Deciding these efforts were futile, we drained our borrowed gas and tried again. There was no hope.

I was concerned about Luella. I was expected home Saturday night. She did not need this concern about my well-being added to an already over-burdening mental load. So we re-fuelled the plane. I volunteered to stay behind, and Bob was finally able to get away to let Luella know that I was still alive. Getting out proved to be an exercise in its own right since we had landed in such a remote area.

I had bought the plane shortly before taking this trip. Someone had removed the compass and we hadn't replaced it yet. Thus we had no navigation aids. In those days even science fiction writers hadn't dreamt of G.P.S. (Global Positioning Systems). In our wild ride we had become thoroughly disoriented. Our point of landing suggested that our flight path must have described a vast "U". Edmonton was not anywhere near where we were headed!

After Bob left, my hope for getting out rested with a provisions crew that was to bring in supplies to the fire-tower by track machine. A road was to be built in that area and provisions for the advance party were to be thus provided. My host, whose meagre supplies I was helping deplete, was to be provisioned during the same trip. Monday came and went; no freighters. Tuesday came and was about to go when finally the awaited team arrived. What a relief to be taken to a bush camp by the road! Wednesday was to see my deliverance by truck, but another rain determined otherwise. Thursday we managed to reach High Prairie.

The bus for Edmonton was to leave during the night.

My education suffered a slight upgrading that night. I had come to regard alcohol as an unmitigated curse and here it was being sold long past what I regarded as a reasonable closing time. I dared to share my sentiments in the matter, but the hotel management obviously wasn't about to alter its ways at the behest of some intrusive transient. So much for bylaw reform!

When I got back to Edmonton Friday morning, life was supposed to proceed, but I wasn't quite certain of the path. Years before, I had embarked on a summer school program that was to produce, first a teaching certificate, and later a Bachelor of Education Degree. During the early fifties there was still a shortage of teachers which had carried over from the war years. To address this problem the Alberta Government had established a summer school program that would enable a person to gain a teaching certificate during three summer sessions. Having had a considerable amount of teacher training during my four years at Prairie Bible Institute, I felt that an additional six- week session would be adequate for a beginning.

By the time I indulged in the aforementioned flying safari, I was well into my B. Ed. Program, so I set that summer school program aside during the summer. The previous winter's experience seemed to clearly indicate that some knowledge of Cree and a flying license would be very helpful. Things hadn't gone well in the matter of language learning. The flying had distracted me. I doubted that our instructor could even speak what he was supposedly teaching. (As it later turned out, when the locals at Little Buffalo heard my teaching tapes, the dialect being taught was from Ontario, quite useless in our area.) Since I had gained little, there wasn't much to lose. Having lost a whole week in the matter of language study, direction in that area was easily discerned.

What to do about the flying was another matter. My father had discouraged it, and aren't we to obey our fathers? Furthermore, Luella had experienced extreme stress during the previous year and I didn't see how I could, in fairness, add to her burden by engaging in the hazardous lifestyle of a bush pilot. For her sake I was prepared to pack it in. But, to my great surprise and relief, it became apparent during that Friday when I returned from Trout Mountain, that she believed I would likely carry on with my training. With that discovery, the reconsideration process was cut short. Yet I had lost a whole week in an already tight time frame.

Yes, we had certainly done one cross-country flight. (Most people settle for a sedate little jaunt to several nearby airports.) But I still needed the balance of my forty-five hours flying time, a cross-country solo, a written exam and a flying check out.

Having survived the trip north, I decided to go to Regina, Saskatchewan. In later years I would have hesitated to do such a thing but inexperience is a great promoter of self-confidence. I will pass over the details of that trip other than to comment on the great emotional drain involved in early flying. Fortunately I was strong. Having put that hurdle in the bag, I successfully took the two required tests. I was now a private pilot.

True, there were still some supplementary courses to be taken, but I was on the way, or should I say "in the air." I flew CF-ELC (Echo–Lima–Charlie) for twenty-five years during which time I experienced one bruised knee. Surely my guardian angel must have been one of the most alert available. Oh, there were incidents, to be sure; at times I didn't expect to do more than provide a few lunches for some roving bear.

Two early incidents helped to launch my career. Our landing strip was just off the Northland Mission yard, so I would park "Evangeline," known to Transport Canada as CF-ELC, in the yard. In later years I learned that the proper order is: flip the prop, then release the tie-downs. On this particular occasion I had that order reversed. I must have had everything else right though, for when I flipped the prop, a mighty roar ensued and Evangeline was on a roll. I rushed to the door and tried to activate the brakes with my hands. Unfortunately, plane brakes were designed for feet, not hands. Brake application is not a matter of a simple push, as in cars. The brakes are on the rudder pedals and a twisting action of the toes is required. Of course, what I should have done was flip the magneto switches but there was a great brevity of time. Mr. Ferguson's bunk shack and a power pole were only a very few yards removed. Total score? One pock-marked bunk house, one dinged wing (It had caught the power pole.) and one abbreviated propeller, the remains of which still bravely chewed at the bunk house.

In due course things were set right, by which time we were the proud users of a fine metal prop—which in its time also produced a few stories. But they must wait, for I'm still trying to get to the beginning of my story.

Yet before that happens I must relate another early experience. One of the bits of wisdom that I had garnered was that for winter flying you must decrease the flow of air over the air-cooled motor by applying tape to the front of the cowling. I was going to try for the bank in Peace River after school. Time was always at a premium so I made what preparations I could before school. It seemed cold that morning so I proceeded to reduce the size of the entry ports with the suggested tape.

Long before I was anywhere near the Peace River Airport the plane was heating badly, but walking was not an option. During the subsequent motor job, the intensity of the heat generated became apparent. The metal in the cylinders had begun to run. Thus did one become wiser in ways of the flying world. Oh, I became a dedicated user of tape, but learned to curtail my enthusiasm.

Chapter 2
New Lives Begin

During the late teens of this century, there was a small family living in Russia. The serenity of the lives in their little segregated farming village had come to a severe end. Life had been good, but the agonies of the Russian Revolution changed all that. Prior to the Revolution, the Mennonite communities established under the auspices of Queen Catherine had prospered greatly. The lands were fertile; the czar regime was tolerant if not benevolent; religious and educational liberties were enjoyed. Not only did the agrarian society flourish, but likewise did the manufacturing and other industries.

Unfortunately, ease and prosperity tend to breed forgetfulness. It seems that a degree of smugness, arrogance and intolerance had wormed its way among the supposedly pacifist, humble peasants. Thus when anarchy swept through the land, the Mennonite "islands " became easy targets for marauding bands which looted, burned, raped and generally terrorized hapless victims.

My parents were among the fortunate ones who survived the mayhem and the later period of starvation. Mother recognized early on that there was no future for her family in Russia. I believe her primary concern was the spiritual well being of her family. Dad was a true farmer thoroughly wedded to the soil, fine horses, and good equipment, but in time his early reluctance to leave all was overcome.

In fact, before their train passed through that final portal at the border he was sweating so badly with anxiety, he was worried the money bills Mother had sewn into his shirt would become apparent. Somehow the overland train trip and the ocean crossing never rose to prominence during later retelling of my parents' stories. I suspect that any inconveniences suffered during those times of transition were relegated, either consciously or unconsciously, to a closet of forgetfulness out of profound gratitude for a deliverance of inscrutable proportions.

The route of the emigrants involved, first, a trip to Moscow where they were screened for physical problems. Then they were taken overland by train, to Riga, on the Baltic Sea. There they were checked once more for health problems. Eyes seem to have been a principal target. Many people's eyes were damaged during the tests. Seventy-five years later, Sister Mary still speaks with feeling about her experiences there. Two aspects of her stay in Riga are fresh in her mind. A pleasant memory involves a precious pair of black boots she received there. A less pleasant memory remains regarding the eye tests emigrants were subjected to. For a reason that remains a mystery, the health inspectors either checked or pretended to treat the eyes with a solution that did permanent damage to at least some of the eyes thus treated.

From Riga, the emigrants were taken to Liverpool with a small steamer. There they were transferred to an ocean going vessel which took them to St. Johns.

In time, they arrived at Herbert in Saskatchewan. There they began to slowly reassemble their lives. If the Liberals ever wanted to gain a solid voter, they got one in Dad. I suspect he

Rear: John, Mary, (Mary's husband, Isaac) Helen, Jim
Front: Henry, Mom, Pete, Dad (1946)

voted one way all his life out of sheer gratitude without so much as considering their policies. The fact that they had made it possible for him to come to Canada was all that was required to keep him on side.

One matter of great concern to him was the matter of raisze-schult (travel debt). The nearly destitute immigrants had received advances to cover their passage. Once here, some tended to forget "the pit from which they had been dug." Not Dad; to him it was a priority item that his travel debt should be paid. Dad had a true horror of anything dishonest.

During those days, visiting the neighbours was still a much practised art. Four items of conversation were dominant as the smelly kerosene lamp offered its feeble inspiration: genealogies (Surely, according to Cousin Waldo, our great grandfathers had at least traded tomcats away back when.), the raisze-schult, experiences in the *zenitaia** and life in general back in the beloved motherland. We children were always obliged to miss juicier parts of the conversations. The high point of our evening came if and when we were asked to go to the damp cellar for a round of apples. Making a new beginning was not easy. There were language and the other usual immigrant-type difficulties. These once prosperous people had been all but wiped out financially. Then, as if all that wasn't tough enough, their first and last fine crop for many years was hailed out.

They resettled at Tugaske, some sixty miles northwest of Moose Jaw. There Mother had a church group, thanks to the efforts of such dear people as Uncle Ben and Rev. Bueckert who, in the midst of their poverty, farm struggles, and lack of training, kept a flame alive. This dry, desolate and destitute scene, in time, witnessed my arrival. Matters of that nature were never discussed in those days, but years later I was interested to meet

**One aspect of the agreement under which the Mennonites settled in Russia, stipulated that, in lieu of military service, male youth would be obliged to give three years of service to the country. Usually this involved work in reforestation camps maintained by the Mennonite community. During wartime some of the men served in Red Cross type work at the front lines of battle. This effort was known as the "zenitaia"*

the midwife who presided at the occasion.

Somehow we survived those years of the "thirties" which have been well documented. It was not easy, however. We had our share of frozen water buckets, pillows that had to be warmed by sitting on them, toilet seats which would cause other seats to crystallize, snowstorms which could make you lose your way between the house and the barn—all the fine things of early life on the Prairies.

Even though we needed her badly, I was relieved for Mother when she could, at the fairly young age of 52, leave all the misery behind. Mother was often ill but I have not one memory of her complaining about anything. What torture it must have been for her to have to visit that snowed under outhouse or to get up in the dead of winter to build a fire in our frozen kitchen stove and then to venture out to the barn to milk. In those days it seemed to be understood that those were the tasks that women did.

Thus we were not surprised when one early spring afternoon, while we children were out playing on a frozen pond, Dad took her to Tugaske where she caught a train to the hospital in Moose Jaw. I suppose we waved as the open bobsleigh softly glided over the silent snows. Mom likely suspected what was coming, but did not want to disturb us. Certainly it was not a matter of her being unconcerned about her children.

Several weeks later I was awakened one night by the passing of our Model T Ford on the road not far removed from my bedroom. Dad had been summoned to receive a message at the Wilson Hartels, who had the nearest telephone that worked. Fearing the worst, he had first gone to get my sister Mary, who was then living just down the road. Together they had gone to learn that Mother had gone on to better things where cold, misery and suffering gain no entry.

How fittingly someone encapsulated her life in her epitaph when he inscribed, "She died as she lived, in peace!"

I was fifteen at the time of Mother's death.

Some years previously I had girded my loins and joined several older siblings on their almost three mile trek to our local centre of learning. Our quest for wisdom and understanding must be spoken of as having happened in a "hall of learning." One must be careful to use the singular, for it all happened in one room—eight grades, one teacher, and not an aide in sight!

I made my debut official with a cuss word on the first day. Thanks to some remarkable teachers, we progressed through our eight years at Winfield School. We didn't know what a library was and never heard of a gymnasium, but it didn't occur to us that anyone could go through school and not know how to read. One of the brightest experiences of those school years was the arrival of new readers. What a joy to have books to read!

As I think back to those years, I marvel at the degree of contentment we enjoyed in our poverty. I cannot remember feeling deprived at the time. If, in retrospect, I were to feel deprived, it would be in the matter of books. During those childhood days I would have had time to read, and how I would have enjoyed that. During later years, when books did become available, there was never enough time for them. But many or few books, there is not a person on earth with whom I should have liked to exchange places, past, present or future!

Officially Winfield offered Grades 1 through 8. Thanks to Mrs. Ward, I managed to add Grades 9 and 10 by correspondence. Mrs. Ward lived in Tugaske. In winter she stayed in the teacherage which occupied one end of the school building, but during the warmer months she would walk the seven miles between school and Tugaske, morning and night. There was no talk of teacher's aides, secretaries, preparation time, duplicating machines or a dozen other amenities. She, and others like her, simply got the job done.

Certainly the attainment of success in that setting involved a good deal of sweat on the part of students as well. My older brother had gone off to Ontario to work, among other places, in a tire factory. He endured that for a brief time before returning home. He arrived home early one morning. I was in the barn milking. On the floor lay my geometry book. I was trying to get those theorems into my head. In time I believe I mastered all forty-eight of them; 24 in grade 9, the remainder in grade 10. Both teachers and students understood—success entailed work and real effort.

It is strange what remains in one's mind after fifty years. When I help Luella make the bed, I am still often reminded of the "envelope corners" that we were instructed to make in our home economics course. Having acquired wisdom in such matters, the time came when new horizons met the searching gaze.

The 1948 crop was a disaster. Dad and my younger brother, Peter, were spending time in B.C. by then, so it fell to my brother, John, and me to scratch together a few sheaves and thresh them. We didn't need a threshing crew. Having attended to that matter, I struck off into the wide world as I understood it in those days. Somehow I found my way onto a grain farm southeast of Regina. There I hauled grain with a half-ton pick-up from a half-pint combine. When that task was done I left for an area northeast of Yorkton. There I pitched bundles for three days. The fellow wanted to give me ten dollars per day but such extravagance was too much, so I negotiated for nine. Maybe he felt this lad had to be loosened up a bit so he offered some booze during settlement.

My next stop was at the Bowhay Ranch, near Airdre, Alberta. I got in seven days of pitching bundles there. As a field-pitcher, it was my job to go from rack to rack helping each teamster load. The other field pitcher was from Ontario. He took time to visit while the 16 year old kid slaved himself. That seemed unjust. At any rate, I was making $8 per day. Unfortunately, I left all $56 earned in the hospital in Calgary along with the end of my index finger. I don't remember ever having missed the money but the finger could have served me well these past 50 years.

The finger incident occurred just after we had completed the threshing and just before we were to go to Calgary. The lady of the house planned a chicken supper. Would someone lop the head off a rooster? Sure. While my accomplice held the wings and legs, I held the victim's head with my left hand. As I was bringing the dull axe down with calculated enthusiasm, the handle caught the ground. As a consequence we went our separate ways; the rooster to attend to rooster-type affairs, and I off to Calgary, with some haste, catching the drips in a bowl as we went.

The finger should never have come off because the piece was still attached. When the doctor gave me the options of feeding the segment to the cats or facing the possibility of another trip to the operating room, I, with my usual carelessness, opted to feed the cats. One of the consequences of this experience was the acquisition of my new designation, "Pointer." The part of the finger left to me was uncomfortable for some time to come. To ease the situation I would walk around with my left hand at my belt. Not a great deal of imagination went into my new name which I acquired at my next stop.

For years various preachers had been convincing me that I should be "born again." I stubbornly refused. One excuse I gave was that when I decided for Christ I meant to make it stick. I decided to postpone making a commitment until I went to Bible School, reasoning that there my wobbly spiritual legs might be somewhat stiffened. Another lad, by the name of Penner, must have had a similar philosophy. When good old Rev. Unruh gave the opportunity for a commitment, the other fellow and I were ready. I quietly made the suggested arrangements. Christ took my sins and I took the new life that He offered. Who would want to back out of a deal like that? Not I; I've never considered it. That is not to say the halo hasn't experienced a few smudges, but the cleansing blood of Christ is great on smudges just as it is on the original sin account.

Next summer I was at summer camp at Lake Peltier south of Swift Current. There someone showed us some slides. One of these was of two Indian graves, alone in some forsaken prairie. The speaker wondered about the destiny of the souls represented by those two mounds. I did as well. I have tried ever since to make people's souls, especially Native souls, a matter of my concern.

I doubt that the camp leaders were much impressed with anything I might have said or done in connection with my newfound vision and reason for being. That very night, when campers were supposed to be quiet, I went on a straw throwing tear. Sanctimoniousness didn't come naturally to me.

Having completed the winter in the Swift Current Bible School, I returned to the old home place which John and I looked after. By then Dad had remarried and moved to B.C. with my younger brother and new stepbrother.

I had not settled in my mind what to do next. One afternoon I decided to build a snow machine. Most snow machines in those days had skis and were driven by propellers. Mine was to be a motorized toboggan. Propulsion was to be by a large flat wheel with cleats. Having very few materials and less tools with which to work, I soon became disheartened with the project and set it aside as infeasible, or better said, impossible. I resolved rather to get serious about completing high school.

It was as well that I went into high school with a degree of resolve, because a steadfastness of purpose was required. Tugaske High School was over five miles from home. School buses were unheard of, so I was on my own. Being on my own meant riding my bike over the gravel road in summer and riding big old Tony in winter. Tony was a great big grey gelding designed for towing farm implements, not for riding. He was not a member of equine aristocracy but he got me there. Sometimes when the temperature approached –50° I would spend the night in the janitor's room in the basement, eat pork and beans, and stay warm. Charlie Stevens kept a cot in the furnace room. When I travelled, which was most of the time, I froze my face with great regularity. I don't remember ever staying home on account of the weather, or for any other reason. When I reached Town I still had half a mile to walk after leaving Tony in the livery stable. (The last time Luella and I drove through Tugaske, both the barn and school were gone.)

There was another good reason for resolve. Our high school was not designed for laggards. Grades 9–12 were in one room with one teacher, Ernest Dyck. He must have been a patient man. There were no semesters or any other labour saving devices. A simple formula prevailed. If you want to pass—work. So we tied into our nine subject workloads and worked. There wasn't any provision made for fun, games, and malarkey. Everyone knew judgement day fell during the last days of June when we were obliged to write final examinations provided by the Department of Education. The mark obtained at that time determined the final mark. There were no provisions for picking up missed courses. If you fell short, you repeated the whole year. During my final year, I stayed home from school for the last week or two before the exams. I got up early in the morning and forced myself to spend all day at my books. I didn't study on Sunday, but to make up for that I was up shortly after midnight to prepare for a Social Studies test. Looking back, I can only conclude that I wanted to pass. My efforts paid dividends; I did pass.

News of my passing grades reached me while I was working on a gravel crusher preparing gravel for the road between Banff and Radium. For several reasons I was happy for a few moments of respite from my task on the conveyor that took unprocessed material to the crusher. It was good to learn that my many weary trips to school—plus the even more wearisome hours in the books—had been rewarded. It was good to be off that conveyer for a spell too. The job was really dangerous. I was obliged to stand on the framework of the machine with no platform or escape route should a large rock leave the belt. I can still see that one large rock coming at me.

It seemed to edge closer to my side of the belt as it waltzed over every roller. I saw it coming, but I had nowhere to go in a hurry. Jumping into the boulders 12 or 15 feet below me was not a healthy alternative. Sure enough, just as it got to me, it jumped off the belt—grazing my hand with which I clutched the heavy angle iron framework.

It's strange how clear the memories associated with that job are: the cold, damp tents; the drunk shovel operator creating a stir early Sunday morning; my partner losing his job partly because we couldn't agree about whether the magnetic and the geographic poles were in the same place.

Other memories still linger from those days of knocking about from job to job and place to place. When I see quiet homes in the evening, lit and serene, I am reminded of those lonely nights when I would be trying to hitch a ride and none would be forthcoming. I suppose I felt just a bit envious of those who could be quietly and comfortably at home while I was out alone looking for a lift, and failing that, a dry place to sleep. And even yet, when I drive I like to be warm. It seems I never quite forget how unpleasant it was to be told, "Well, this is as far as I go." That was my signal to get out and face whatever the weather happened to be doing. I still have a soft spot for anyone with his thumb out.

The autumn of 1951 rolled up on the calendar and life was scheduled to roll forward. My buddy, Henry Dyck from Swift Current days, had persuaded me to join him at Bible School in Three Hills. This began my 42 year sojourn in Alberta. The big move originated at the old home place. The departure involved neither fanfare, tears or a U-Haul. I walked out to the highway with my suitcase and caught a ride. One who bade me farewell was my dear little niece, Shirley Andres.

I will pass lightly over the four years spent at Prairie. The lad from Saskatchewan had much to learn. Those were memorable years, never to be forgotten, never to be set aside. I will be eternally grateful that I was able to experience the training offered in that setting, but the details seem not to fit here. Were I to seek to recount them the story would become too long. There would be details about studies, friends, summer work, student work, conferences, special ministries, faculty and staff. The task of telling that story is likely better left untouched, but one fact should be recognized. The whole experience contributed to the wobbly resolution occasioned by the lonely Indian graves mentioned previously. Foremost among the lessons inscribed upon our consciences was the idea that each of us is indeed our brother's keeper.

Interestingly, as I review my life I find that when I was at a fork in the way, there was often a friend to make a suggestion. As graduation approached the logical question was, "What now?" This time Allen Bienert had words of wisdom. He told me of the six-weeks teacher training program that the University of Alberta was offering. After four years of heavy studies, many of which had to do with the teaching of children, a six-weeks program sounded just right. U of A it was to be, come July! That allowed me several months for further training in a lumber camp in B.C.

Penny was a wide spot on the railroad east of Prince George. If you wanted to go somewhere you either rode on the railroad or walked on it. One Sunday we missed the first option so we had to employ the second one in order to meet a commitment to hold an evening meeting in a nearby town. I rarely eat dates without remembering that 25 mile stroll when we used dates as fuel.

My training at Penny included a four week crash course in the perversity of human nature. My job as bull-cook furnished me with some eye-opening insights.

One of the memories seared forever on my mind is the remembrance of the impressive sunburn I acquired just before leaving the camp. The winter's snows had been just a little too much for one of the bunk houses, causing the roof to collapse. My job involved getting up early and tending to the fires. Thus I was ready for a nap on a fine sunny afternoon. The bunk-house, open to the heavens, seemed a most inviting place for a nap-suntan combination. Well, talk of a sunburn! When I left my job, I set out for the Vancouver area first by rail and then by thumb-express. One of the rides I caught down the Fraser Canyon was with a brewery truck. The lad must have been late for supper because he certainly wasn't sparing the horses around those corners. I, for my part, was holding on to my seat for dear life trying to avoid rubbing my aching back on that seat. I was only partially successful. I was certainly relieved to reach Hope from where the travel was more sedate.

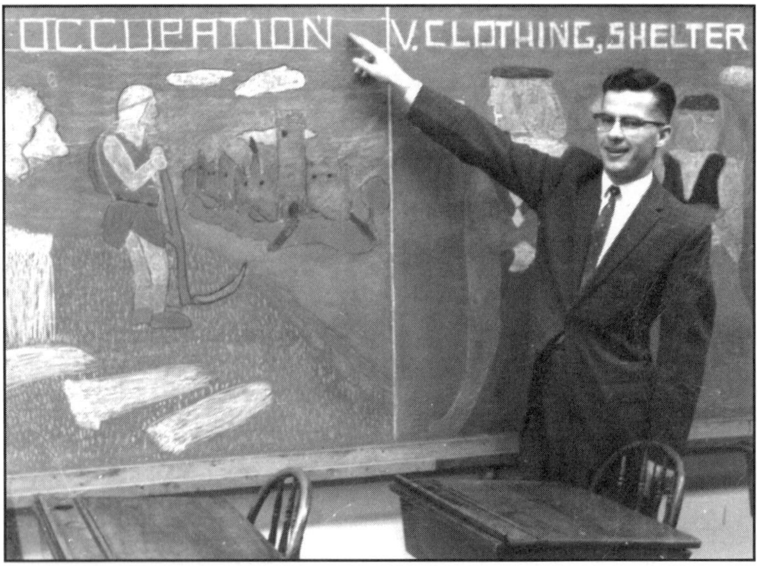

Teaching at Prairie

Chapter 3

My Teaching Career is Launched

The summer of 1955 came and went as did the session at the U of A. When the new school year approached, I was ready to take my first teaching position. There was no hassle; I got my job.

My school was in the midst of a triangle, the vertices of which were Breton, Drayton Valley, and Buck Lake. To get to my new home, I rode the oldest railway passenger car then in existence. No wheels fell off, however, so it got me as far as Breton. Had it been dark, the conductor would, no doubt, have lit the kerosene lamps that still adorned the coach.

Likely suspecting that a long, lonely year was about to begin, I was in no hurry to go out to my school. Instead, I chose to help some local lads build the rodeo corrals at Breton. When the fellows saw me wield the post maul they observed that I would do okay in the strapping department. It seems that the "strap" featured prominently in their perception of education. As matters turned out, I pounded a lot more home runs than children.

When I arrived at Meadowdale, I found my school three miles removed from Buck Creek, an oil gathering facility surrounded by the homes of the work force. Most importantly—where one lonely teacher was concerned—someone in one of the business establishments dispensed the precious mail weekly. It's hard to remember how much I appreciated Luella's weekly letters.

The town-site was built as the oil development progressed. Meadowdale predated the village. Meadowdale School was a unique structure. Its walls were of varnished logs with a cottage style roof. The single classroom was heated by a huge wood-burning furnace. It was a very attractive place set off nicely by the surrounding bush.

I was to teach Grades 1–8. Just in case that wasn't a great enough challenge, I decided to do it in the midst of the Pembina oil patch where people came and went with astonishing frequency and regularity. There were up to twenty-nine students. As many as nine might be in grade one and helpless. During my two years there, I processed some 60 students.

My most advanced instructional aid was a piece of chalk. No one had ever heard of a duplicator. There was no thought of additional help. Furthermore, I was expected to devise a book rental system. I was to take in the children's own books, allow a certain value for each text, put the books into rental sets, and rent them back to the children. Nor let us forget the Christmas concert. The community demanded it.

Housekeeping was a do-it-yourself project which transpired in a teacherage cobbled together from two bunk shacks joined by a type of entry. Somehow I survived. Maybe the whole scene was a disguised blessing. I doubt that anyone ever heard me, during the next 36 years, complain about inadequate facilities or resources. Furthermore, it is likely the children learned something.

In later years when teachers had the benefits of so many amenities, I tried always to remain appreciative and thankful. The salary scale reflected the appreciation of my efforts. During my first year of teaching I earned $1900.00.

An interesting item in retrospect is the matter of discipline. The children were just plain decent. I fail to recall anything that might be considered a discipline problem.

I believe I was the last teacher at that school. After I left the children were bused out and the school itself moved to become a museum. I've never seen it since.

Chapter 4

Concurrent Proceedings—A Bond is Forged

Many years prior to all of the foregoing, my brother, while on a singing tour, visited the home of a noteworthy young lady. When he came home, the report he delivered sparked my interest and I made a mental note. Several years later I made a trip to Swift Current to hear the Janz Quartet sing. While there I was introduced to that same young woman, Luella. I continued to carry a mental note—while she remained unencumbered by any memory of me. I had to jog her memory some years later.

During the summer before I began teaching, I managed to meet her again. This time we had some time together over a piece of pie in the Sun Café in Meadow Lake. I'm sure Luella wondered about all of this. The course to be followed was obviously much clearer to me, nor did the vision wane. My setting, back there in the bush, miles from nowhere, was one to stimulate the imagination in matters of the heart. Having no car during that first year did nothing to ease the situation.

During our encounter in Meadow Lake, Luella agreed to letter writing which we then did on a weekly basis. Now sentimentality is not really one of my salient virtues but letter day was a red-letter day during that period.

One Saturday I hadn't yet received my weekly letter. As a diversion, I decided to go look for a moose. The snow was deep and I, being less than wise in the ways of the wild, walked much too far. By the end of the day my left knee had given out; I could scarcely drag myself to the road. Fortunately I managed to catch a ride. The logical thing to do would have been to go straight home, but sentiment overcame reason—and I dragged myself over the three miles off my route home in order to obtain the anticipated missive. Luella never let me down. If and when my knees ache these many years later, I am reminded of that day and caused to wonder if that long walk is the reason.

By Christmas 1955 the letter writing had generated enough steam to seemingly justify a visit. Having travelled as far as

North Battleford where my oldest brother, Jim, lived, I was well on my way. Whether due to sympathy or Cupidistic inclinations, Jim offered to take me to Barnes Crossing beyond Meadow Lake. He couldn't take me all the way to Luella's because of drifted roads. In any event I was getting close, so off I trudged across the wintery landscape. The grapevine must have been in good order because I hadn't gone very far when a horse-drawn caboose approached. Luella and her dad had arrived to give me a lift.

I must have been one of the original live-in boyfriends because once at Luella's home, there was nowhere else to go. Mind you there were, as the song went, "Maggie's" mother, her father, her sister and her brother. But sometimes I did get to see "Maggie," (rather Luella) alone.

One of those rare occasions was a bright moonlit night. The others had gone to bed so Luella and I went for a walk down by the still and frozen creek. I don't put much stock in stars being in their right places but that night the moon was. Years later, after she had overcome some of her bashfulness, Luella told me that it was that night when something clicked.

My second year at Meadowdale was more pleasant than the first. I bought a Studebaker car. With it, I could at least get out on Sundays when I would rotate between Breton, Drayton Valley, and Buck Lake. But I was well beyond weekend travel distance to Luella's. She was teaching near Loon Lake, in Saskatchewan, many hours removed from my scene of operations.

The following summer we agreed to both attend summer school at the U of A. It was time to act. For some reason the planned moonlit setting in a canoe on a lake west of Edmonton didn't work out, so I settled on Queen Elizabeth Park as a suitable place to ask my pressing question. Years later I pointed out the park to a group of Meander River students, while we were on a field trip, noting the memories. Were they excited! I had been too. To think that Luella was going to be all mine, "to have and to hold!"

But that holding part was going to have to wait. The next year, during which I taught grades 9 and 10 in Paradise Valley, also passed. After spending the following summer at the U of A, on the 15th of August at 3PM, having completed our examinations, we set off for Meadow Lake to make good the promises of the previous summer. Brother Pete had joined us by then. Off we roared in "Little Black Sambo" who was always an enthusiastic

Luella & Henry married 1958

participant in the activities then. (We didn't understand about political correctness in those days).

Mother Friesen had been dutifully making wedding preparations. On August 17, 1958 it finally all came together. I didn't have to wait quite 14 years for my bride, as did Jacob of old, but I came a close second. The bonding that Rev. David Friesen applied, a procedure witnessed by numerous well wishing friends and relatives, really took. It has held for over forty years and shows no signs of cracking.

Our honeymoon was a rather extended excursion which took us as far as the Mexican border. We were turned back at that point for want of passports. In any event it was time to head north. Fortunately, the American officials observed our thwarted attempt to visit Mexicalli (border town between Mexico and California) and let us back into the U.S. For a few moments we wondered how this was going to work out. The Americans have this thing about people wandering in from the south. In due course we arrived at our first home—a basement suite in Hanna. Hanna was where we were to teach for the next two years. Luella taught grade 2, while I taught some 35 grade 7's.

It was in Hanna that Arlyn came to join us on October 15, 1959. Now we were three. Things were falling into place, but it was quite apparent to us that this setting was not to be ours for long. Neither did our next stop suggest permanence.

When we were at Hanna we had contact with Prairie Bible Institute at Three Hills. During our second year at Hanna we were invited to come and teach grade 6 at Prairie while their regular grade 6 teacher took a sabbatical. Moving was no big deal. We may have made two trips with Sambo.

I had a good year with those grade 6's but Prairie was not the place for us either. We needed more elbow room. We did not wonder long about where to find it. Our next move became apparent during spring conference—but before we continue with that part of the story I should mention an incident which could have called for an entirely different script.

Thoughtfulness and gratitude cause us to consider the, "What ifs?" of life. One of the more thought provoking of these occurred during our year at Prairie. Only Arlyn was with us during that trip as we set off to spend Christmas with Luella's family. We were going east on Highway 9 when we came to an unplowed section of the road where there were only widely spaced ruts in the deep snow. Because our Volkswagen's wheels did not correspond to those ruts, the snow caught us and threw us off the road. When the car nosed into the snow, which filled the ditches, it upended, landed on the roof and rolled over onto its left side. During this procedure, the left front door flew open and most fortunately came to rest forward under the left front fender. I say, fortunately, because I was thrown from my seat and had come to rest with the front doorpost across my chest. I was unhurt, but how different the outcome might have been had the door come to rest in the more normal position! Neither Arlyn nor Luella was hurt either. Our spirits may have been dampened somewhat by a lowered roof and spilled diaper water, but surely, gratitude should have been the official reaction. (In those days, for rather obvious reasons, diapers were soaked between washings, in water.)

Spring Conference brought to Prairie visitors from the world in general. But we weren't interested in the world in general; we were interested in Canada's north and its people. The message and the invitations from that quarter were delivered by Margaret and Graydon Dennis. They needed teachers for their two-room mission school. Would we be interested? I *guess* we were interested! All those years of preparation were finally coming into their own. We were prepared. We were ready—and I believe I should add that we were eager!

Chapter 5

Little Buffalo—Our Hope, Our Home, Our Mentor

The next instalment of our lives was beginning. It was to be a short twelve-year period. I don't remember the Little Buffalo years as seeming long. Sometimes our visitors inquired about the length of our stay. Almost invariably, regardless of whether the answer was three years or ten, the reaction was, "How can you stand it?" meaning the isolation.

I can't remember ever being anxious to leave. We became a part of the community and were settled in our minds that we had found our place. Looking back at that time, rather than feel that we stayed too long, I would be inclined to wonder if we couldn't have done a little more, if I couldn't have done it all a little more kindly. From the present perspective that 12 year period seems a small thing. Twelve years it was to be, though, and I am satisfied that our time-frame was complete when we left. How disappointed I would be now if I felt that we had deserted our post!

At this point I would like to introduce the reader to the home that adopted us. The Little Buffalo settlement, sometimes referred to as L'Hirondelle, in honour of one of the original settlers and traders, was about 70 miles, by road, northeast of Peace River Town. Little Buffalo Lake was a small shallow reed and grass impinged lake. To the south, about five miles, was Lubicon Lake. It was larger, deeper, and generally more significant. The word "Lubicon" was likely a derivation from "Laboucan", Chief Laboucan having once lived in that area.

One of the original settlements in that area was Matawasaw. In our day Matawasaw was basically a ghost town inhabited by only one family. The settlement was decimated during the flu of 1919 when people died at such a rate that those left to bury the dead couldn't keep up. They stacked the frozen bodies for later burial. The few people who remained, scattered. One such family was the L'Hirondelle family. Josie and his family moved beyond the west end of Lubicon Lake and there established what came to be known as, "The Farm." On his farm Josie raised cattle and ran a fur trading post.

Northeast of us was another little settlement with two trading posts, Andy Colson's and Harry Lambert's*. Northwest of us about 12 miles, on the trail to Peace River, was a third settlement, Cadotte Lake. The traders were all Metis. Though no one seemed to concern himself unduly with matters of blood, the community was divided fairly evenly between Metis, and those with Treaty numbers. We had to make a distinction in our school records.

Generally speaking, settlement into that area had been from the south. Little resettlement took place during our time, but before that, those who had moved in had come from the Lesser Slave Lake area. The senior L'Hirondelles had come from St. Albert.

Before 1950 there was no school in our region. The children were generally taken out to the residential school at Grouard on Lesser Slave Lake. Being less than satisfied with this arrangement, the people were open to the idea of a boarding school in the Little Buffalo region. The Roland Smiths entered the picture at this point. The Smiths arrived in Peace River by train in May of 1948. They rented a house on Kaufman Hill and established an office on the site of the current Toronto Dominion Bank.

The Smiths had planned to go up the Mackenzie Highway in order to establish a mission but they were intercepted by Raymond L'Hirondelle, son of Josie. Raymond, by way of making a case for a school, had compiled a list of 66 students in his area. He was in a good position to be thus informed because he and his Dutch war-bride were partners with Josie in the fur trade.

Using his Bombardier (a track-mounted vehicle), Raymond took Roland on a tour of the region. They visited Cadotte Lake,

**I fail to recall, even an inquest, into Harry's death. Surely he deserves at least a mention here. Harry kept horses at Runaway Lakes, several miles off our trail near Three Creeks. During one trip to Peace River, he left his wagon with his furs on the trail as he went to check on his horses. When he returned to his outfit, it was to find someone stealing his fur. Shooting followed. His large belt buckle saved the thief from Harry's shot, but Harry was killed.*

Big Buffalo (Bison) Lake, Haig (Fish) Lake, Marten River, Weasel Lake, Loon Lake, Little Buffalo and Prairie Lake. Little Buffalo, being quite central, was chosen as the site for the new mission.

Mr. Smith relates that the school began to function in 1953–54. Their building, a 16 x 20 foot log structure chinked with mud, doubled as a dining room for the children.

Because of failing health, the Smiths returned to Ohio in 1957, but were thrilled to visit Little Buffalo in 1988 to witness the first Grade 12 graduation there. It involved three students (Jane Sesequin, Elaine Jobin, and Veronica Whitehead). During those early years the whole operation could likely best be described as being of a modest nature, but there was progress. The buildings which emerged continued to be of log construction. Boys were accommodated in a building with staff living-quarters at one end. A T-shaped building housed the girls and their supervisors. The older girls were in one area, the younger girls in another, and the supervising family in the third branch of the T. Clothes were stored at the point of intersection. Several smaller out-buildings were provided for additional staff.

By the time of our arrival in 1961 a frame building had been added as part of the Mission complex. It housed the generating plant, the washing facilities, the tractor and a vehicle. In a slight concession to modernity, ancient boxlike telephones furnished communication among the buildings. When a tense situation arose, they were a source of reassurance. A two-room frame school had also been built. This was a government venture overseen by the Peace River School Unit.

The whole arrangement seemed quite satisfactory. Parents could leave their children when they left for their trap lines. Teachers were paid by the School Division which also maintained the teachers' accommodation and school. The Northland Indian Mission* received a small allowance from the Division for each child. As for other staff, they were expected to raise their own support among interested friends and churches.

**See Appendix A*

Aboriginal women scraping moose hides prior to tanning

Chapter 6

We Move In

After many years of preparation, both as students and as teachers in southern classrooms, Luella and I were ready to do what we had set out to do. How pleased I am that I could cut my teeth in southern classrooms where I learned to assume "kids is kids" and I could expect them to learn regardless of minor variations in skin pigmentation. Our family at that time included Arlyn who had been born in Hanna. The other three children joined our family during the Little Buffalo era.

We moved toward our new life with expectancy as well as a certain excitement. Certainly no one could have anticipated what life was to involve in this "foreign land." We were happy that we would be in this new setting far removed from the tedium of normal life on the outside.

Having motored to Peace River, we were met by Graydon and Margaret Dennis, directors of the Mission. As so often happened in later years, we spent the night at their house. Together, but in separate vehicles, we drove out to Little Buffalo the following day. This first trip was interesting but uneventful.

The first 20 miles got us as far as Mrs. Oslie's store at Three Creeks. Then the bush trail took us across Dry Meat Creek, past Twin, Simon, and Cadotte Lakes, through the pines, over a few prairies, and finally home. The trip seemed long, but then it always did. Nowhere in the bush could one ever really relax and just drive. If nothing else, one was at least approaching another curve.

Seeing our new community for the first time, as we approached it from the north, was a singular experience. We arrived in early autumn when nature had assumed it's pre-winter attire. She was a lady of high fashion having in her wardrobe a sensational outfit to go with each season. Her attire for the occasion of our arrival was certainly no disappointment!

There was not a great deal of time for reflection during our arrival but a later experience will help to explain how things were. During a rare unhurried summer day I found myself on the slight rise of terrain north of the settlement. Situated to the south and at a slightly lowered elevation was spread a scene of unusual quiet, tranquillity and beauty. Little of human activity was evident but nature's triumphs were very much in evidence.

Trees and willows, flaunting a hilarious cacophony of hues, were interspersed with lush meadows. To the right slumbered our little lake, its blemished visage camouflaged by the intervening distance. Though justifying no profusion of superlatives on its own, in this setting Little Buffalo Lake was a jewel properly set. The heavenly arches furnished a most appropriate canopy.

I fail to recall any trumpet blasts or fancy carpets being used to herald our initial arrival. Likely there were none. We proceeded to unpack our Little Black Sambo, not a vast chore, and move into our temporary home. We shared these quarters with fellow tenants, the mice. These freed themselves of any obligation in the matter of rent by entertaining Arlyn. He would lie by the cellar hole and appreciate their antics in their lowered arena.

During that first year we would often take our meals in the dining room, along with the children. We remained in the log cabin for only several months. Later that fall a prefab, two-bedroom teacherage was brought in and assembled.

We appreciated getting a new home but did have to sympa-

Little Buffalo school and teacherage

thize with the poor wretches whose misfortune it was to shingle the place at –40°. Even though the house provided was of modest standards it compared favourably with my first teacherage at Meadowdale.

We were not expecting any degree of elegance, but thought water piped into the house would be helpful. At an early opportunity one of the local fellows, Raymond Scotty, dug a trench to the nearby dugout. Into this we laid a plastic line which enabled us to pump water into a barrel in the attic. Gravity provided the pressure. Thus with the help of a propane water heater we had hot and cold running water. Later we got a well, but the water was so rusty we were left thinking the smelly, bug-infested dugout variety hadn't been so bad after all. At any rate the problem of sun tanning was eliminated. All one had to do was take a bath; no Sunscreen required.

Moving in and settling in are two different matters. We had done the former and planned certainly to do the latter. We never planned to have our bodies at Little Buffalo with our hearts elsewhere. One of our first duties was to make known our presence. At the same time we suggested people might wish to send their children to our school. With this in mind, George Dunn and I did visitation. Our advances were met with some reserve. It was during one of those visits that I learned my first Cree word, "Moya," which meant "No."

The utterer of that word later became a dear friend. Surely he had many good reasons to be less than thrilled to have us come into his life. His idea of child rearing was to give his son a gun and some shells, send him into the bush and let him learn to survive. Here we were, on the other hand, representative of a new day—harbingers of the unfortunately inevitable.

Had their people not got on well enough without our books, schools, and intrusions? Surely there was evidence aplenty that their child rearing methods worked and were in many ways superior. The child referred to in the previous paragraph, for example, learned to survive on his own and became a first class bushman.

He and I could wander all day in the bush. By that time the only two directions of which I was certain were "up" and "down." Not Peter; when it came time to go home he would strike off in a certain direction and walk straight to our pick-up. Or when we were out hunting, before I was even aware that there was a moose in the vicinity, it would be dead meat.

As I look back, I hope we evidenced no arrogance, yet how could we have seemed other than arrogant to those good people? We saw the old way of life as a fine system which had to pass with the changing times. Was it not becoming an impossible situation for increasing numbers of people to live off shrinking wild life reserves? Wasn't modernity pushing in from all sides? Weren't the children of that and future days going to need 20th Century tools with which to cope?

Adjustments were required on both sides. There was going to be a lot of learning and re-learning. For us, our first year was to be a year of many varied experiences. It was to be a most eventful year during which our mettle would be gauged and our commitments challenged. The children were going to learn and, yes, even adults.

The Cree, who are most adroit at getting it correct the first time when they judge a person's character, have a special name for an outsider who has a lot of learning to do. He, to them, is a

Flossy, the Shetland pony, entertaining the kids.

"Moneow." Normally this term is taken to mean "White Man"; what it really means is "greenhorn."

How green and awkward we would-be-teachers must have seemed to a skilful and intelligent people! We were learning, though. It seemed hardly a week went by without some major upheaval.

Much of what was new to us involved running a boarding school. This dimension involved responsibilities and people not normally encountered in an ordinary day school setting. The day did not begin with books nor did it end with them.

In Peace River there were books to keep, supplies to purchase, errands to run and hospitality to be exercised. The latter was not a small matter. After some of us had been in the bush for a few months we were highly primed and often ready for a good visit. It fell to the lot of the Dennis' to listen to our stories while we sounded off until well past bedtime. I don't remember ever being much aware of isolation, but I do remember being ready with a few stories when we might have gone to bed.

Out at the Mission there was much for our small but dedicated staff to do—the usual domestic chores were compounded several times. Meals needed to be cooked, dishes washed and clothes patched. Children needed supervision, though they played quietly when they had free time and weren't busy with their chores.

As for discipline, it was not a great matter. Even then the children were considered well behaved. By today's standards they were wonderful!

Some might wonder if our boarding school effort fits at all into the sordid picture of some residential schools that has been recently emerging. I make no apologies for our efforts. If in some instances we seemed strict, or demanding, it was for the children's long-term good. Certainly, we encouraged the use of English, but there was no danger of the children losing their Cree on that account. Language was not a major issue.

The little people were amazing in this respect. Some might come to us in the fall with very little English. By the end of grade one they were usually fluent, able to progress with reading and school work generally. This, of course, was our purpose. We wished to have them progress in their subjects. In our books it was a kindness to give our students the freedom of movement and association which fluent bilingualism would facilitate.

As for the sex problem, I can't imagine such a thing ever being even a temptation to our staff. For one thing, most of them were married. Furthermore, I'm certain that their minds were not inclined to such thoughts.

The matter of God was more difficult. People of Christian persuasion, by their very calling must, if they are to be consistent, take a position dictated by the Scriptures. To do otherwise precludes being Evangelical. Having adopted the Scriptural belief system, the Believer feels he has an obligation to share God's revealed Truth. The consequence can be conflict. The situation becomes particularly sensitive in an authority figure/child relationship.

The average anthropologist has few qualms. His position is usually, "Leave them alone; every culture has a right to exist and maintain itself in any way that it pleases." The Christian on the other hand says, "If there is a washout on the track surely it is my responsibility to flag down the train. If there is pain, fear, superstition, a feeling of helplessness and foreboding and I can offer relief, surely it is my duty and privilege to offer hope."

Thus, we did emphasize teaching the Scriptures. I don't have any recollections of the children being unusually restive under this instruction. Maybe one boy's observation can best encapsulate the situation and the relationships.

The trapping families would return from their trap lines in early June and camp near the Mission. The children were understandably excited to rejoin their families. Our Chuffle also left the Mission to join some of his camping kin. Now Chuffle was by anyone's standards neither a sage nor a philosopher, but he did have a certain understanding of matters related to his wellbeing. Before many nights had passed he was back. When he was asked why he didn't stay out in his freedom, his reply was, "I want to eat good and sleep good." Obviously he considered himself neither deprived nor abused.

I believe most of the people conceded what we were doing in our schools was helpful. We, for our part, were assured of our

Billy Jackson, with kids on a softball outing

course. Thus, we went to work gloriously ignorant of the facts of life which became so evident later to all but the most insensitive. We were rather uninhibited by overwhelming concerns regarding such matters as slow learners, dyslexia, hyperactivity, whole language, sight reading, new math, political incorrectness, and a host of other methods and concerns which later came to occupy such an important place on the educational scene. We just taught school assuming that if we started at the beginning, worked systematically, faithfully and hard, the majority of our children would progress. Luella taught grades 1–3 that first year and I grades 4–8.

The only time we missed days of school was when we were obliged to go to a convention. In later years Mildred Mallinger and I went to an in-service at Keg River. Mostly we just taught school. If the fuel stopped flowing, I might carry it in with a tin can and feed the heater, but the school remained open for business.

In time we were proven correct in our innocent endeavours, for our children learned. When the time came for students to move on, they could take their places in outside classrooms and hold their own. Apparently Shirley L'Hirondelle led her class in Peace River and her brother, Chester, was near the top too. Recently another ex-student mentioned in his public lecture that he was pleased to find himself well able to compete in Jr. High after leaving the Little Buffalo School. Some of our students have remained in the area to become leaders in their communities. Others are ministers, business executives, tradespeople; the kind of mix you would expect to emerge from any small rural two-room school. Billy-Joe Laboucan is almost finished his Master's degree. Randy Jackson is a lawyer. I continue to be proud of our Little Buffalo people.

To be certain we were on the straight and narrow, we had superintendent visits. Two of them bear mention. The first transpired during our first month or two of school. I don't recall how I learned that we were being visited, but in due course I wound my way down to the lake to communicate with our visitor. Some lakes have sandy beaches; some don't. Ours didn't. What it did have was a wide margin of grass and reeds. Now I have no idea where the dear man found his float plane to hire, but there it was on the lake side of the marsh. I took my position on the shore side. I assume we had a learned, albeit, high decibel exchange.

United Nations with our famous International

Apparently all was considered to be well on the educational front. With the termination of our shoptalk session he departed, hopeful, no doubt, that his next visit might be in environs better suited to learned discourse.

The other superintendent's visit which merits mention occurred years later. The dear gentleman, and a gentleman he was, came to us in the dead of winter. How long he expected to stay I know not, but his visit went well beyond the usual. He stayed at our house for about three days before his plane came to retrieve him. I wondered whether teachers received merit points for their wives' good cooking?

Being far removed from the normal concourse of school affairs we dared to put the wellbeing of our children before normal protocol. Since the trapping families, whose children we kept, might be as far as five wagon-trail days removed, there was no way the children could join their families for such normal school holidays as Easter break or Thanksgiving. Nor was there much for them to do at the Mission during those times. Thus we taught through such holidays, as usual, banking the days. We then shortened the school year by that number of days.

School became a tribulation in June. The classroom became unbearably hot, yet to open the windows was to invite hordes of bugs. We put in an order for screens, but the matter must have seemed of urgency to no one but ourselves. We waited four years for those screens. During the intervening Junes we sweated, scratched, swatted and endured.

Another difficulty associated with trying to teach in June was trying to get our scholars back from their respective families' tents in the morning. The nights were cool and very pleasant, so pleasant in fact that no one wanted to go to bed. Light was no problem, for darkness never came—only a heavy dusk. Though our own children went to bed, their sandbox might be occupied until eleven o'clock or longer.

Furthermore, the freshly returned and reunited families which camped near at hand must have had much to relive with our students. The whole scene was more conducive to socializing than learning. For this reason we were happy to abbreviate the school year by using our banked days in June. Unfortunately, officialdom eventually became aware of our errant ways and caused us to teach, sweat, scratch, swat, and endure.

Chapter 7

Our Memorable First Year

As the first term at Little Buffalo progressed, something of a routine emerged. We learned what was expected of us. There were no major upheavals before Christmas, except the session we had with Arlyn.

Because Luella was teaching, we needed baby sitters for our two-year old. We regret to this day the one instance we thought he would be okay without one. He was sleeping one Sunday night so we dared to leave him for a time while we paid Dunns a short visit. When we came home he was sitting on the couch wide eyed and concerned (but not crying). His immediate question was, "Did you see Jesus?" His explanation for our unexplained absence seems to have been that we might have been raptured. Normally, Luella was always there for the children even if I was often gone.

Usually Mrs. Vandenbogard looked after Arlyn while we were in school. This system worked quite satisfactorily as long as he was well. We hated taking him out of the house, however, if he was ill. Once when he was ill we were obliged to take him regardless. During the day he had a fever convulsion. We knew nothing of such things, so we rushed to the hospital in Peace River. We felt badly about leaving him in the hospital so we obtained medicine and took him home. Our problems were not over. When he had his next convulsion we were really frightened. We had never witnessed anything like it. We immediately turned around and took him back to Town.

This problem was, fortunately, one of a kind. During the 12 years when we were far removed from medical assistance we had hardly a serious health problem, nor even a broken bone, except for one which didn't really count. I will write about it later, when I relate the events associated with our Co-op field-trip to Bonnyville.

Whatever degree of serenity we may have been experiencing, came to a sudden end in February. Saturday was town-going-day. Usually we needed freight for both the store and the Mission. There would be the eagerly awaited stack of mail plus personal-order items for our staff and the community.

On this particular Saturday a vehicle exchange was also to be enacted. Dunns' Power Wagon needed attention so it had been left in Town. Dunns had used Dennises' car for the trip home. We were to exchange the vehicles, since the Power Wagon was ready.

The term Power Wagon may need some clarification. This machine was a Dodge creation, one of the original 4x4's. It was a machine of no mean proportions. It boasted enough motor to pull a house, had a great high cab, rode very high and had a picket-type box. These features translated into a machine which could do wonders in some circumstances and was a disaster in others. One year when our tractor was unavailable we used it to put in our crop.

Although it was certainly not our policy to miss the regular Sunday morning church service, on this day we did because we had been detained in Town Saturday night. Sunday morning dawned as a fine, clear, crisp, winter day, though not cold. We set off early for home, choosing to go by the shorter, steeper route up Kaufman Hill. The other route was up the highway in the second valley over. (The highway has been rerouted since then due to the instability of the slopes).

We had no problem on the hill, but once we were on the straightaway we had a major problem. We believe that the front wheels may have slipped into four wheel drive. If the driver, in that event, decelerated, the heavy front end would slow faster than the back end. The road was glare ice. Whatever the cause, we went into a skid, hit a great wall of snow which had been pushed up by the snowplow, turned over and slid forward on the roof. Sliding thus, the cab filled with snow which caught and held me in a most undignified head down, bum up position.

Dignity was, at that time, not an overriding concern. I remember two fleeting thoughts, "If Luella is free, I may get out of this; if not, 'Lord here I come!'" With that I went out. I remember no fear. Never before or since have I lost consciousness. I had suffered no blow. I was unhurt except for two minor cuts but

I was out cold. I'll ask Luella to tell the story as it unfolded.

Arlyn had been standing on the seat between us, but shortly before the accident I had set him on my lap. However, I must have let go of him when I blacked out as I felt the truck turn over. Whether I was out seconds or minutes I don't know, but the first thing I became aware of was Arlyn's crying. I felt like I was in total darkness, and closed in all around so I couldn't move. To this day, I don't know if it was only my state of mind or if I was really packed in by snow. In any case, I struggled to free myself, and light returned. Somehow I got Arlyn and myself out through a broken window.

Henry's condition looked hopeless; he was packed in snow head first, with only the bottom of his parka and his legs and feet sticking out. I clawed at the snow, but it was so firm I couldn't possibly remove it by hand. It was more like ice. I had to get help, but I didn't know which way the closest farmer lived, so I opted to go back towards Peace River. Arlyn was too heavy to carry, and too young to walk fast. Groceries were strewn over the snow, so I plunked Arlyn down on a sack of flour and told him, "Stay here till Mommy comes back." (Years later, a Three Creeks resident told us he had happened by and wanted to take Arlyn with him, but he refused to go). Several times I started to leave, and then went back to the truck, torn between going or staying. I needed to get help but then again I was afraid Henry would die when I left him alone. I walked down the road till I met a car. The driver gave me a ride back to the accident scene. He didn't think he could do anything either, and made a remark to the effect that Henry was probably dead. As Arlyn and I went with this man to seek help, all I could think was that if Henry was dead I would take Arlyn and go back to my Mom and Dad.

Somewhere down the road we met a tractor with a front-end loader. The men tried to lift the truck, but it wouldn't budge. Then they began shovelling the snow away to dig Henry out. With the first shovel-full they almost caught his glasses. It turned out his body was bent at the waist and his head was not where we thought. What a relief it was to find him still alive, although unconscious! The men put him on the back seat of the car to take him to the hospital. On the way, he shivered so violently, he al-

most fell off the seat. He began to regain consciousness and kept asking how Arlyn and I were. By the time the doctor saw him, he was trying to joke, "I'm like Elvis Presley—all shook up." The physician looked as if he was concerned about Henry's sanity. He was also concerned that he might develop pneumonia because blood plasma had seeped into his lungs, so he kept him in the hospital for five days. Arlyn's account of the story took very few words in comparison to mine: "Truck fa(ll) down. Daddy in the (s)now. Lanny cry."

After several days in the hospital Henry was free to go home—just in time to see Rev. Ferguson's cabin go down in flames a few days later.

The reader may be interested in our road. It wasn't a road really, just a glorified trail. Some effort had been made at creating ditches. They were ineffective in serving a ditch-like role, but were very efficient when an unfortunate wayfarer slid into one.

Since a tow might be three days in coming, one planned his own policy of extrication. Once, when my vehicle wouldn't come out of a ditch, I mounted one set of wheels in the groove created by wiring two poplars together with clothes hangers.

During another session, when there happened to be a tow available, we had a problem getting the pulling vehicle onto dry ground due to the length of the mud hole. We tied slender poplars together end to end to give us the distance required for pulling.

For such trails as we had, we owed our gratitude to the oil companies: Shell, mainly. I doubt the government spent a dollar on that road until the 60's. The originators of our lifeline to the outer world had matters other than comfort, speed and safety on their minds. One wondered if the original trail blazing crawler hadn't merely followed some errant moose, out for a summer stroll.

While the frost remained in the ground we could drive with relative ease. Though snowplows were not thought of, we could continue driving. Even when we had heavy snowfalls the snow was not a major problem. The wind never blew, so we had only to deal with what fell, no drifts. The preferred method of dealing with the snow problem was to mount a blanket or piece of plywood under the motor compartment. This kept snow from burbbling into that area as it did without such precautions.

Normally when someone was on the trail, others would be aware. If a traveller didn't show within about five hours of the assumed departure time, others would go out looking for him.

Telephones were even more unthought of than snowplows, but we did have some radio contact. Scheduled time was at noon, but we could never rely on that system. On clear winter days we could expect the radio to work, but it was then we could expect the road to work too. The radio had an irksome tendency of bringing in what we didn't need and failing when it was needed. Even though I never discovered where in B.C. Honeymoon Creek is located, we were sometimes well entertained by the messages. During times such as the spring equinox we had no roads—and no radio either.

One of the earliest lessons that the newcomer did well to learn was that the trail was not a joke to be taken lightly. Dangers on it were a stark reality and one had better gain respect quickly.

One of the most significant facts of life was the matter of spring break-up. Break-up was expected in early April. Well before that time it was of utmost importance that fuel, groceries, vehicles and people be in place. There would be no vehicular traffic for the remainder of the school year. When the last supply vehicle disappeared into the bush one had a strange feeling, even if only momentarily.

Having vehicles in place sometimes meant having one vehicle parked at the airport. It was required because the Peace River Airport is nine miles out of town. Dennises were very good about taxiing, but we didn't always want to trouble them. Also having a vehicle available at the airport meant we could drive south in the summer. During the summers I would, sometimes with a great sense of relief, tie the plane down for however long we stayed out. I could, for that length of time, happily settle for a conveyance that maintained contact with firm earth.

Our isolation during our first break-up period was total. We had no plane, no airstrip, no telephone, no mail, no fresh food, no medical help and no police, but we did have our God and that made all the difference.

The Mounties had a Beaver aircraft stationed in Peace River but it never seemed to do us any good. Usually we couldn't even contact them. Once when we could have used outside intervention and got through by radio, it was only to learn that the plane was in Victoria, B.C. Never, to the best of my recollection, did we get police help when we really needed it.

Though the presence of God left Spork tasting much like Spork we always felt protected in the areas that mattered.

If there were those among us who despaired of ever eating anything other than Spork again, we were in due course rebuked for our unbelief. The sun shone, snows melted, the trail softened, the creeks flowed, bridges failed, washouts occurred—but then the sun continued to shine and the procedure was reversed, with a little human intervention. The natural beauty all around us mitigated the fact our isolation was complete, if not in fact, then at least in perception. When the greens of spring appeared, our community became a beautiful place once more. Winter offered fine scenes, but nothing compared with the verdant greens of spring.

By the middle of June 1962, the cooks were rather hard pressed to discover what else might be done with Spork and peanut butter. We were also curious regarding what might be in the mail. I, being the uninitiated lad on the block, decided that surely I should be able to use the trail by then. George Dunns again graciously allowed me to use their power wagon which had been repaired after our February mishap. Off I went.

Going out must not have been a problem; maybe the ground was crusted by frost. Washouts and bridges had been somewhat restored by Josie L'Hirondelle and his men. Josie went with a tractor and wagon when it became possible to do so, taking out his furs. But he had the benefit of experience.

My coming back with groceries was another matter. Though dry in sections, the whole distance was a series of mud holes and washouts. Maybe I was too careful, but I certainly didn't want to wreck Dunn's truck a second time. Had I blasted along I might not have gotten stuck quite as often.

The script of this melodrama read something as follows. Hit a mud hole. Conclude that maybe I was merely stopped. (Surely I couldn't be stuck again; I'd come only 600 yards since the last hole!) Not prepared to face reality, I took half measures. These would insure that I was indeed stuck. Out would come the jackall. Hopefully, some sticks were available to support it in the mire as I tried to raise a wheel. Hopefully, other sticks were available to lay under the wheels, and hopefully, not all four wheels needed to be replanted. Finally the moment of truth would arrive. If my work was up to standard, I was ready to move on to the next hole. If not, I started over. By this time I was spared the uncertainty of whether I had a real problem or not. At least darkness was not a concern. I could work all night—no problem.

When the locals undertook these projects they would be more philosophical. They would go prepared with extra food, extra time, and a tea-pail. I couldn't be bothered with such finer things of life. I believe the only time I ever built a fire was the time we were trapped in the overflow on the Peace River. But I have become gaunt on numerous occasions.

Even days—and nights—on the trail come to an end. After 18 hours of the procedures outlined above I reached home, bringing to an end a memorable trip. By then I was prepared to concede truck travel was problematic. But surely with a tractor and wagon one could pass. A week later I tried that method. Coming home the second time over those 50 miles of trail took about 24 hours of relentless effort. There had to be a better way!

These trips occurred during the first June after the February snow-bank incident. At that time, while I recovered in the hospital, Luella spent several days resting at the Dennises. Then we went home. After Luella got home she did not have the opportunity to ride in a vehicle for the remainder of the school year. None of us was aware how severe had been the impact on her, of the hopeless session on the road while I was in my precarious situation. This became apparent later, when we tried to travel.

Since I wasn't yet flying, Budd Dennis came for us with his plane at the end of the school term. He was one of the first pilots to try out our new strip. Our plan was to fly to Peace River, drive to Edmonton, and then on to Saskatchewan for a visit with Luella's family. Then we would return to Edmonton for summer school.

Budd's plane was a four seater, so Luella and Arlyn got into the back seat while I sat up front with Budd trying to garner a few flying tips. I quite enjoyed the experience, being totally unaware of the mental agony Luella was experiencing. Some people might have screamed, causing the mental pressure to dissipate; but that isn't Luella's way. She just keeps quiet and absorbs the whole impact, likely to have incidents recur in future dreams. One can only imagine her relief upon disembarking in Peace River.

We spent the night in Peace River and in the morning set off for Edmonton. The car trip was a further session of mental torture. Luella had the fearful sensation that the car was veering off the road and heading for the ditch. Somehow we arrived in Edmonton and spent the night.

Next day we headed west on Highway 16 planning to reach Meadow Lake that day. Again the severe mental torment returned. I drove slower and slower, but nothing helped. By the time we reached Elk Island Park, we had all had enough. We turned around and went back to Edmonton, abandoning the visit.

Fortunately, time heals many wounds. As years progressed, most of those irrational fears subsided. Luella still experiences fear, but when she does there is a reason. Now she does her own driving, taking extensive inter-provincial trips on her own when I can't join her. I'm quite proud of her independence.

There were many other nerve-wracking experiences during that first year. The result of all these pressures was not positive for Luella's nervous health. I didn't wish to further torture her with the many uncertainties involved in my flying. Because of this concern I seriously considered abandoning the idea of a plane, especially after the Trout Mountain experience I related earlier. On the other hand, it seemed very important that I learn to fly. We didn't want a repeat of that first break-up period when we were helpless and vulnerable.

During that summer we devoted our attention to several matters. Luella was content to spend time at our suite with Arlyn. I, as indicated earlier in this account, planned to learn how to speak Cree and fly a plane. The degree of my optimism became progressively apparent as the summer progressed.

There were other consequential events during that never-to-be-forgotten first year. They must, however, remain in the files of our minds. Luella and I agreed long ago that if there was ever to be a book it was not to come at the expense of the desired privacy of others.

Henry with Evangeline (1963)

Chapter 8

Time to Fly

During the previous summer when we had been driving west from Edmonton for a little vacation near Jasper, we stopped at a campsite. While we were there a small plane flew over. The idea occurred to me , "I wonder if we shouldn't have one of those up north?"

Now, a year later, having experienced a break-up period followed by those two very difficult trips, I was satisfied a plane was what was needed.

If there was to be a plane there had to be a landing strip. Near the Mission was a small prairie which we proceeded to plow up, work down, and seed to grass that spring. Our equipment was a tiny grey Ford tractor, a mounted plow, a log float, and not much else. These tools served reasonably well up to a point, but they did nothing for the unfortunate rises and depressed places in the terrain. We would have to live with them.

The ground rose slowly to the north and then dropped off rather suddenly. The crest of the rise was about two-thirds of the distance from the south. Both approaches were guarded by trees. Only cold-sober pilots need apply. At any rate, the mixture of grass seed took hold, developing a base on which we could rely even in the wettest weather.

Next, flying lessons. Upon my arrival in Edmonton I discovered the Edmonton Flying Club and one of their instructors, Bob Stanton. He was one of a kind, who in his other life was the local sheriff. Bob assumed responsibility for this would-be-pilot in a philosophical fashion. The only concern I recall him addressing head on was the matter of his cigar ashes; I was to do my turns properly so the ashes would not be scattered by wind entering the vents at the base of the wind screen—a condition brought on by improper rudder use.

I started off on Cessna 150's with their tricycle landing gears. Bob did not consider them a viable machine for the flying I would be doing. When we went shopping we discovered CF-

ELC, a fine little Cessna 140. This plane had the desired tail wheel, plus skis. With the advent of ELC I forsook all others. I have never cared to fly anything other than that remarkable little craft. It served admirably.

My moment of truth was not long coming. One evening we had been doing circuits, at the Edmonton Municipal Airport, when Bob asked me to pull onto the apron. With that, he got out and announced, "Okay, put her on her top, if you like!" On that cheery note, he shut the door and strode off. I was on my own!

Surely one of the loneliest places on earth has to be the cabin of a plane under such circumstances. Up I went; that was the easy part. But once up, I knew that rule #1 was fully operative; "What goes up, must come down." Furthermore, I wasn't the only kid on the block. Sometimes one might have five planes ahead of him, each needing to land. How many there were that night I don't recall. Life just then seemed demanding; radio, controls with which I was barely acquainted, gravity, a tiny plane, and a very firm earth with which I was supposed to become reconciled peacefully, if possible. That was one time when I did have a knot under my belt. But somehow the incident came to pass with both the plane and my neck intact.

Most of what we did during our lessons was a routine practice of various skills required, but some of our manoeuvres never became at all routine. We would fly west of Edmonton, well away from populated areas, climb to 6000 feet, and practice stalls and spins. The theory is that stalls, spins and spirals don't necessarily happen only to the other guy. If you happen to get involved, you had better know what to do— and quickly.

I found these manoeuvres, to use a subdued term, taxing. I am flying along; I cut the power. Suddenly the roar is replaced by an eerie, almost-silence. I pull back the control column. The silence is shattered by the outlandish squawk of the stall horn. I'm slowing down; I stop flying; the nose rises for a short time and then suddenly plunges, I'm headed for a scowling Mother Earth, and the fact that she is 3000 feet below, is only somewhat consoling. "Left rudder!" shouts Bob. I shove left rudder. The spin begins. Don't let the spin become a spiral! Spins are benign; spirals tend to be fatal. "Okay, right rudder! Back on the control column."

Apply power. Right rudder ends the spin, while the backward pull on the control column causes the elevator to bring the plane back into a flying altitude. The free fall after the stall, plus the application of power has restored flying speed. And the power (Thank the Lord for power!) enables me to again resume normal flight. "Whew!"

Those lessons were spooky but, having taken them, I appreciated the experience. As a person deals with a stressful situation successfully he gains confidence. Having gone *beyond* the call of what is normal, one is more confident and relaxed *in* the normal.

I have recently taken a few hours to train my team of horses for driving. The principle I use is the same as the one used in training pilots. I'll refer to my team as Bonnie and Clyde. Bonnie is the pregnant one, and Clyde is the submissive understudy. Clyde was an unbroken colt who worried about a multiplicity of concerns including his own shadow. He was, therefore, dangerous and untrustworthy. Taking the advice of my advisor who knows about horses, I "sacked him out" the other day. The idea is that if the horse is subjected to extreme stress, but not hurt, he will then be able to handle surprises which come to him during routine use, without reacting dangerously.

Not realizing that I was to hold onto him during this procedure, I tied Clyde to a post and presented him with my Fiji sports shirt on the end of a stick. The shirt was light enough to blow eerily in the breeze. This, to him, was an unmitigated horror. He did everything but have kittens. In time, the relentless ropes and exhausting snow in which he fought took their toll and he began to understand he was not being hurt. By then I could snap the shirt at his legs, drag it over all parts of his body and he stirred not a bone. This procedure may never to be repeated because he is now a much steadier animal. Hopefully those wicked kicks, which fairly whistled, are never going to be repeated either. I hope that soon I will have an animal on which I can safely depend.

When I left Edmonton with my shiny new license close to my heart I had merely covered the basic chapters of the flying manual. Other chapters were to be added—the self-help variety.

Do you recall the time I should have left the tie-down ropes on a little longer? Did I mention the time I broke a skylight with my head during turbulence? Or the time when the propane torch threw scary amounts of heat? Or the time darkness closed in on me as I came down from Fort Vermilion, before I even knew where Little Buffalo was located in that vast bush, or the time, and the time. . .? The incidents go on.

As one considers these flying incidents he is left wondering what might have been. The variables are numerous and had they come together in a different manner the consequences could have been entirely different. What if there had been a gas leak? What if I had been detained another fifteen minutes? What if the frost on the wings had been a little thicker? What if that thunderstorm had moved a little differently? In any of these situations the outcome could have been dramatically different and pathetically unfortunate.

People in our church congregation were no doubt a bit surprised when I announced—before Luella and I sang—that on my 66th birthday I felt I was something of an authority on Divine intervention. I am very conscious of the fact that the days which I now enjoy are an unanticipated bonus.

Chapter 9

Health, Homes, Happiness & Help

In this chapter I wish to meld into one the concepts of home, health, happiness and my contribution thereto as I provided transportation. Transportation was indeed a crucial ingredient in this equation for it provided access to health and therefore to a happy home.

One of the first "homes" that I should like to mention is our own, including something of how our children entered into the picture and how they fared once they arrived. Some will wonder how life worked out for them in their minority status.

As indicated earlier, Arlyn moved into Little Buffalo with us. Laurella, Lyndell, and Lanna-Marie joined us later and in that order. Each little "moneow iskwiis" (white girl) or "naapiis" (boy) was greeted warmly and with great interest. (We still smile at little Karen L'Hirondelle's observation when she first examined Lyndell as he slept in his crib. Her comment, after a thorough study of the little fellow, was "Big Hands!" Her astonished

CF–ELC (Evangeline)

exclamation almost awakened the already nervous little fellow.)

Often when older white children move into Aboriginal communities there are adjustment problems. Our children never experienced that difficulty. Starting life in that setting was good for them. Certainly our children were members of a minority at Little Buffalo, but we were never aware of any rejection. There was more apt to be a problem in their being overly deferred to.

Once Luella caught Arlyn, as a pre-schooler, standing on the front step giving instructions to the children at play in the school yard. Giving instructions seemed to him a family prerogative. When it was explained to him that authority invested in the parents did not necessarily devolve to the children, he accepted his demotion. There was never a repeat performance.

Generally there was genuine respect and appreciation all around. In fact, when Arlyn went among white children and was expected to play with them, he felt strange. His explanation was that he found the Native children more kind.

Kindness was a highly esteemed virtue in those circles. There was certainly no point in trying to fake it, but if a person were considered " kind" you had it made. To be considered kind was the ultimate compliment.

We give the Native influence of the Little Buffalo Community credit for some positive aspects of our children's personalities. It was Arlyn who spent the longest time among them and benefited most. For instance, it seems that it was from the Cree that he learned his unusual perceptiveness, where human nature is concerned.

One of the pleasures in becoming acculturated was to participate in the bannock and dry meat diets that were common. Also, when Laurella put her dolls to bed, it was apt to be in the hammock-style swing used by the neighbours. Two ropes are hung from opposite walls of the cabin, sagging to within a few feet of the parents' bed. Flannelette sheets are draped over the ropes to make a pouch into which the child is laid.

This was an intelligent arrangement. At night the parents had only to reach up with a sleepy foot to give the cradle a swing. Also, in later years I discovered that the confining pressure of a sling can bring real comfort. (I had experienced a broken collarbone when I was thrown from a truck as it was trying to dislodge another vehicle stuck on the streets of LaCrete. In an effort to keep the bone segments in place, we used a harness which proved very comforting. Not only did it keep the bone ends from grating, but it also created a comforting, secure sensation.)

When I brought Johnny Halcrow's baby home from the hospital, the parents didn't come for her for several days during which time Arlyn grew quite fond of her. When she was taken away he missed her and asked that she be replaced. We have her tooth marked autograph on the crib to this day.

It is not surprising that our children became comfortable with the local people. Even I who have seen a few white folks in my day, emerged from years of isolation to discover that the outside folks had not only acquired anaemia but they had also learned to speak with American accents.

At hearing a knock on the door one day Luella sent one of the children to check. Soon Laurella was back in some awe, "It's a white man!" She was so flabbergasted that she left him waiting on the step.

One only needs to listen to Alexa McDonaugh of the New Democratic Party for 25 seconds to discover that health care is a matter of some concern to many Canadians. Some people become concerned when they must cross to the other side of their city to go to a hospital. In remote areas people feel fortunate if there is an ambulance available which can get them to a plane within two hours. Then, if the plane takes only three hours to get to Edmonton, they feel that they have been well served. The experience of my teacher, farmer, pilot friend Mel Calanchie would illustrate this point.

One evening he was standing between the bumpers of two vehicles giving assistance on the road when a third vehicle smashed into the parked vehicles with enough force to throw them both off the road. Mel's legs were pulverized. Assistance being what it was, he was enroute to the hospital in Edmonton for about six hours. He had that brush with death but lives to tell the story. Mel did get the care he needed. Thanks to that care, an iron will, and calcium from milk by the gallon, Mel walks.

Arlyn & Laurella with "Evangeline" in the background.

In the bush at Bison Lake there are many little grave markers to indicate health services have not always been available. Of one family in an earlier era, only five of seventeen children grew to adulthood. This situation has changed over the years. Infant deaths are rare today.

Though no one, during our time at Little Buffalo, ever dreamed of a hospital in that area or, for that matter, a nursing station, some measures were taken to ease the health care problem.

When we arrived in 1961 there were only one or two vehicles in the community other than what were at the Mission. Translated, that reads, "Some people had to do quite a lot of driving."

The trail was difficult at best and often impossible. Today a good gravel road puts Peace River within reach in an hour.

The Peace River Health Unit took some responsibility for our communities. Health Nurse Rogne's name appears in Luella's guest book with some regularity. She and others like her would visit the school, giving the youngsters their shots as well as tending to minor woes.

Early on we were given a store of medicines to dispense from our house. Only in a remote and extreme situation would a layperson assume such responsibility, but when proper medical help is not within reach a person is prepared to dispense both drugs and convention. We never had any fatalities but we certainly had miracle cures. The explanation which we offered was that people responded so remarkably to penicillin and the like because their bodies were unused to medicine. One of the problems was to have people complete their dosage. "If I'm well, why should I continue taking medicine?"

As for broken bones and gashes, it is remarkable what nature can do with the help of a few splints and butterfly bandages. When Ron Krause broke a leg we patched him up with splints and whatever. We felt very pleased to be told by the medical people at the hospital that our work was superior.

We did blow it in one or two instances. My run-in with our Lister power plant would be a case in point. At one period, during its tenure of service, our one-lung Lister was in a contrary mood. Starting it involved a huge cast-iron crank and some dedicated spinning. Now dedication and spinning a diesel require both breath and stamina but when a certain degree of exhaustion is reached one becomes somewhat ill-coordinated. The consequence of that state was that the crank came off the shaft and smashed into part of the frame with a most unfortunate wallop. All of this would have been fine had not my little finger been between.

Billy Jackson and I expended our most proficient medical skills on the situation, but the pain persisted. We had our Easter break about then. That was the year when I took my family to Meadow Lake before returning to Peace River for the men who wanted to go to Bonnyville on behalf of the Co-op. After about two weeks the finger continued to ache. I began to wonder. Having taken someone to the hospital, I decided to have an X-ray taken of my little appendage. Sure enough, the finger had been broken the whole time. There was no point in getting excited then for it was already well on the mend. Oh, the little fellow is a little dilapidated yet, but it works and there was no lawsuit.

There was another more serious instance. Two of the lads were having a slight difference of opinion in the classroom. I regarded the matter of little consequence and sent them home for lunch. Luella was watching as they left the school. One gave the other a shove causing the other boy to fall. He didn't return to school after lunch but when I inquired of him the answer was noncommittal. After several days I learned that there was a problem. The child's parents were not home and the house sitter had not apparently recognized that the fellow's arm had been broken. After discovering the truth of the matter we flew the poor fellow to the hospital, but by that time the bone had begun to knit. The doctors in Peace River were unprepared to address the situation so they shipped him off to Edmonton where his arm was re-broken and set. Unfortunately, the arm never did become entirely right.

I never had a place in my heart for fighting in anger. That instance confirmed me in my nonviolence convictions. I felt somewhat hypocritical demanding that my youngsters not fight when their heroes, the hockey players on television, accepted no such strictures. It seemed the best way to avoid fights was to keep strict order in the classroom and play with the children when they were having their play periods. Unsupervised idleness makes provision for hassles.

Nevertheless, the memory of another altercation causes me to smile even yet. Early one morning, about five o'clock, someone from Marten River was at the door. There had been an accident and would I fly the victim in? By the time I arrived at the Marten River airstrip the patient was there. Learning of his broken leg, I inquired as to the cause. Oh, he had been "pole jumping." This seemed rather odd given the hour of the day. My suspicions were confirmed by the priest's rather cryptic response, "Kiiyaaskin" (You lie.)

The matter was clarified during the flight. My patient became airsick. In the confines of a small cabin, dietary secrets are difficult to maintain. The resultant odour suggested problems quite unrelated to high-jump poles. About a week prior Ron Krause had broken a leg during a school high-jump event. It seems that my young friend thought that a similar explanation might ease his embarrassment somewhat.

One of the matters for concern during our early years was the problem of tuberculosis. Some of the local people were spending prolonged periods in the Sanitorium or Charles Campsell Hospital in Edmonton. These stays caused disruption in both lives and families. Nonetheless, I am unaware of any deaths due to TB during our time.

Because of the TB situation, a rather rigorous detection program was in place. Periodically an X-ray crew from Edmonton teamed up with the local Public Health nurses and checked both the school children and the general public. If there was a reason for concern, and there often was, we would receive further tests—the needle type. One visit was more memorable than most.

The end of the school day had come; the X-raying was completed but rain was threatening. The nurses were getting anxious about the road. The fellows from Edmonton, however, apparently were not performing up to standard. Likely, that was the occasion for Mrs. Rogne's unflattering categorization of them as "donkeys."

"Donkeys" or otherwise, they had been gone for only a short

time before they were back. This time they arrived as pedestrians. They hadn't even reached the difficult parts of the trail and already they were stuck, four-wheel drive Jeep and all. (The nurses who were driving an ordinary big car managed to keep going for about twenty miles. Mrs. Rogne had been around for a while and normally planned to get on with things!)

The Mission had a little Allis-Chalmers tractor at that time. With it, I set out to help our friends on their way. Strict duty would have demanded that I extricate the men from only the first hole and bid them "Bon Voyage". Rather than abandon them to a certain fate, I opted to continue towing them. After about twenty miles, we overtook the nurses. Their transmission was either gone or going so we chained them into our little caravan. It soon became obvious that this arrangement was not going to work. Transferring the nurses into the Jeep we abandoned their car and set off down that muddy trail. The Jeep had also packed it in by then, so I continued to tow them even over the twenty miles of gravel beyond Three Creeks. Finally we reached the highway at the top of the long hill. In those days, that varia-

The Jackson family "practising" Little Buffalo travel

tion of the present road took one into the town by the River. Once on the decline, we unchained the Jeep, gave it a shove and let it roll the five miles down the hill. Later I discovered that the relieved voyageurs had rolled right into a service station on the corner where the highway meets Main Street in Peace River Town. My own story was more extended. I had those seventy return miles to cover. Fortunately, I had brought a ten gallon drum of gas with me. This precious commodity I transferred to the tractor tank. I was ready to go—and go I did! Mud flew in numerous directions, but that was immaterial; I was going home! Before long my feet were literally packed in mud but that was fine. I wanted only to get home. By the time I got back to the Mission, Mrs. Thiessen was crossing the yard to the kitchen. It was seven o'clock; almost breakfast time. I had some serious sleeping to do. Nine o'clock, school time, came early that morning. If I could get through to noon hour I would catch a ten minute nap and all would be well with the world once more. Admittedly, staying awake was a problem. I stayed on my feet the whole time since it was easier to maintain a degree of alertness that way. It was embarrassing to wake up in mid sentence wondering what in the world I had been saying.

The roll of that Jeep reminds me of another much less fortunate roll. This incident is unrelated to the health topic at hand but is significant in Peace River's history. Our family had been out visiting one Sunday night and we were on our way home about nine or ten o'clock. Looking Peace River way, we noticed a great glow in the sky. This was unusual for we had never noticed such a thing before. Later we learned what had happened. At that time the highway did not follow the presently used valley but one further north. Still, it went under the railway underpass used to this day. A fuel tanker truck had lost its brakes on the long hill. There was nowhere to go but right into Town. Upon reaching Main Street the driver tried to turn left, but the turn was tight and his speed great. The tanker overturned, spilling its aviation fuel down the street. It caught fire and set ablaze three blocks on the west side of Main Street. This was the inferno which produced the light which we saw those many miles away.

Another service, provided for our people, had to do with not-too-serious dentistry. I believe there were some fillings—mostly cleanings and fluoridation. My contribution was transportation, at least in one instance.

By this point in time, a school had been established at Cadotte Lake. When health people came in to visit one school they would visit both. During one such visit we agreed that I would be contacted by radio when the dentist was ready to come to Little Buffalo. I waited and waited until almost dark. Finally the call came. Upon my arrival at the Cadotte strip, I beheld not only a dentist but also an imposing array of boxes and gear including a collapsible chair. Approaching darkness would not allow me to make a second trip. I avoided morning flights whenever I could, but there were three options. We could leave the gear, the dentist could camp on the airstrip overnight, or we could grossly overload the plane. I opted for the last of the three. This choice involved stacking the good man's chattels right up to the skylights. The chair didn't quite fit, nor for that matter did the dentist. Our solution was a compromise. We squeezed them both in. This involved his supporting part of the chair above his head. "Oh well, it will be for only 15 minutes," that is if our steadfast faith in our overburdened little craft was not misplaced.

Government dollars had gone into the Cadotte strip so it was a good deal longer than our Ford tractor variety—and it didn't feature a hill. Takeoff was a real effort but Echo Lima Charlie came through once again. What an amazing little craft! The short flight was uneventful ; evening flights were always silky, but setting the plane down on that short strip was always tricky. Setting it down when so overloaded was doubly so.

One never had the option of a long gliding approach. For one thing, there were the trees, and secondly, there was no length of runway to spare. The hill complicated life even further. Coming in from the north involved setting down on the uphill slope. This incline tended to cause the plane to take off again—not what a person needed when the fence across the south end of the strip was coming at him rather ominously.

While we are on the subject of health care and flying other incidents come to mind. The settlement of Loon Lake was about 40 miles east of us. Their airstrip was beyond the settlement about seven miles. One of my flights involved delivering a passenger there. By this time George Dunns was living at Loon Lake. When I neared the settlement something was stirring on Dunns' roof. Wondering, "What's George up to today," I went in closer. He was busy spreading three large sheets of cardboard on the roof. On them were written the letters, SOS.

Thus rather than turning and going back, I waited at the airfield until the people of the settlement arrived. The problem was that Louis Auger's toddler had fallen on a sharp stick. The stick had pierced his eyelid and gone in above the eye. Would I take father and son in to Peace River for a check-up? As things turned out, the eye had miraculously escaped injury. We could happily return everyone home.

One early summer evening I was out with the tractor preparing our few acres to grow some cattle feed. My peaceful proceedings were interrupted by a resident of Three Creeks who had passed through Cadotte. He stopped to report that there had been a serious accident there. A woman had been hit by a speeding vehicle and thrown high in the air. Would I go and take her to the hospital?

When I arrived, there was a crowd of people around the bed on which she lay. No one seemed quite sure what should be done. She was obviously dead, and there would have to be an inquest. While a decision was being reached time passed. Even though they decided not to send her, by the time I got back home it was 11:30PM and dark. I could still make out the trees but as I went in, I merely made allowances for the fences and the hill. Mercifully, no horses were grazing on the strip. I hadn't allowed for them. "Thank you, Jesus; now I'd sure like to sleep!"

As I continue with this idea of health, homes and family relationships, I would like to make an observation in passing. I wonder if sometimes there isn't a tendency for people of one race to look upon another people and somehow feel that they aren't subject to like hurts; that separation from home or community is somehow less painful; that death is less real.

My observation is that the ties which bound those Native

families and communities together were very strong, and the hurts experienced were every bit as real as those experienced by any people. This closeness of relationships was, in part, a consequence of their manner of life.

Chances were, the home was a one-room cabin. This fact caused the whole family to be together day and night. The togetherness situation was further enhanced by the fact that the cabin was possibly situated in a secluded spot miles from anyone or anywhere. Several situations, which would add credence to this position, come to mind.

One night the parents of one of our families were detained in Peace River over night. Yes, we would keep the children. So Luella proceeded to make them comfortable by giving them beds in different rooms. She needn't have tried. Before long the little folks had made their own arrangements. They were all sleeping in one bed. Being scattered through our small house had been too lonely a situation. They needed the normal closeness.

Then there was the astounding case of Baby Laboucan. Baby Laboucan, who wasn't likely a year old at the time, became ill. My fellow teacher, Norman Dafoe, took her to the Peace River hospital in his Jeep. Because she didn't improve, she was sent to Edmonton. Some days later we received the message that this baby was failing, would the mother please come?

The situation was urgent, so mother and her interpreter daughter went to see the little girl. It seems the visit was all the medicine the little one required. Three days later I was at the airport preparing to fly home when, whom should I see but this happy trio? Could I take them home?

The little one had apparently given up and despaired when she was removed from her large and caring family. When she discovered that she had not been abandoned after all, she perked right up and wanted to live. (This baby is now a young lady. I was interested to visit her and her mother in their home several weeks ago. They live in a new house on the reserve which has since then been created at Marten River).

Uniting families was one of the little perks that gave me pleasure. There was always quite a lot of sickness among the children. Colds tended to settle in the chests. Sometimes we had quite a backlog of little people ready to go home from the hospital. When I brought in another patient and the nurses saw me, their rather spontaneous reaction was, "Could I take this one or that one or, for that matter, two or three of them with me?" Now I'm sure that nowhere in the reams of paper, which is the Ministry of Transport, were my situations addressed but I knew I was sticking my neck out when I flew my overloaded little craft over those miles of lonely bush. I also knew that, if I refused to take the little folks home, it would mean other trips later—and what if the weather deteriorated? So I would agree to take the babies with me on condition that I be given a bottle for each little passenger. Becoming thus involved included the trip out to the airport, reloading whatever and whoever from car to plane, fuelling the plane, etc. When we were ready to go I would plug in each little passenger, pray that I wouldn't go down in the bush, and take off. I can't recall any baby ever yelling during a flight.

One trip particularly stands out in my mind. I was down to just my own bucket seat so that I could haul more freight. I already had a load of cases of canned goods which couldn't be left to freeze. That day when I stopped at the hospital for an anticipated passenger, the nurses wanted me to take an additional two or three. One of the babies was to go to Cadotte, the others to Little Buffalo. I undertook the project with some trepidation. Anyway, by the time I had to take off from the frozen lake at Cadotte I would have burned off gasoline and would be lighter by one body.

As it turned out, no-one was prepared to accept the little girl at Cadotte, so I was obliged to fly the whole load to Little Buffalo where, on skis, we had to squeeze into that short strip. What a relief to tie ELC to its mooring blocks after that trip!

(The word, "skis," in the previous paragraph has a significance worth noting. When a loaded ski plane is brought in, the airspeed must be kept high to avoid a stall. The situation can quickly become critical when the load is heavy and the strip is short and icy. Skis don't offer much braking power.)

Before these digressions I had begun to speak of family reunions.

When the plane appeared after one of these trips, even before it landed, a welcoming party could often be seen to emerge from the settlement. No matter how many kids there were at home, the one returning was a little hero.

During those early years I didn't worry overly about law suits. As time went on they became a concern. I felt I could trust the local people to understand if something went wrong. During our later years, as do-good outsiders began to come, bringing dissatisfaction and dissention, the possibility of a law suit became a definite consideration.

Earlier, I mentioned the strong ties that bound the family together. Those that bound the community were only somewhat less strong.

We who are used to scattered families and frequent moves, find this concept of belonging to a particular region quite inconsequential. As modern transportation facilitates interaction, Aboriginal thinking is changing too, but I recall a track meet involving a number of Native schools. There seemed to be a nervousness, if not actual fear, among some of the visiting students in being found in a strange community. I could only guess at the reason, and my guess was that the concern had its basis in matters other than the historical enmity between the two tribes represented. It seems that spiritual considerations were being weighed.

This sense of home and community is one of the factors which makes a move into the outside world such a tribulation for isolated students and others who wish to resettle. Considering the beauty of the natural environment, the quality of the friendships enjoyed, and the normal closeness of relationships, even the least sentimental among us can have understanding.

Several experiences could be related to this matter. In visiting with one of the old timers at Fox Lake I learned Fox Lake wasn't really his home. That was news to me; I thought he had lived there for 40 years. Yes, he had, but it seems Wabasca was his "home".

At another time, in another place, a Native lady dared to rise during a public meeting to voice an opinion. Someone of a differing view was going to have none of that, "Be quiet, you don't even come from this place!" 17 years of residency were insufficient to give her a right to an opinion.

Josephine & Nora on a shopping spree at
the trading post (1964)

Chapter 10

The Trading Post and Trading Trips

Early on in our careers we developed a certain loyalty to our community. We were there to contribute, and one of the first contributions was to be a trading post. I refer to the business as such because not much money changed hands in the operation. The need, as we saw it, was for a store to serve our little community. Our reasoning was that if a store was available to the people, they would build cabins close at hand, close enough so that when the men went trapping they could leave their families behind and children could walk to school. Obtaining enough staff to run the dorms was always a problem. Nor were we comfortable having to separate the children from their families for extended periods. Whatever the reasoning, an available log cabin was appropriated, shelves and a counter were built, an oil heater was installed; and we acquired a relic of a cash register.

Incidentally, this adding machine was a wonder in ancient technology. The technician punched in the numbers, pulled a handle, waited for the grinding noises to cease and wonder of modern technological wonders, there on the tape was the sum! Talk of crunching numbers! We still have the machine. Unfortunately, on one of my trading trips north, I lost the bolt which secures the handle.

Soon we were ready for stock: pimii (lard), totosaapwee opimii (butter), siiwiniigan (sugar); kiiksiipomiiesowin (morning food), to mention some of the food items. Gasoline, and hardware such as guns, traps and snare-wire were also in great demand. Specialty items like toboggan boards were special order. Oil of Aniseed was used for lynx, fox, mink, and fisher bait.

Only later did I discover that having a good stock was not necessarily a boon. When there is much available the needs escalate. When the needs are apparent, the trader has a problem refusing credit. A hard-nosed trader lets his stocks dwindle when no fur is available. When the fur starts to appear, stock suddenly appears. The ruthless among them can then include booze. Hard-

Henry Enns displays timber wolf and cross fox pelts taken in trade at his trading post.

ships are not difficult to visualize.

The usual routine was somewhat as follows. In theory I was to get the family allowance cheque. Often other pressing needs pre-empted my receipt thereof. Then the family would start spending next month's cheque. Staying within the budget was always a problem. Then when it came time to go trapping I would provide the grubstake. When fur was available, I was to get it— if other needs didn't pre-empt that transaction also!

I had much to learn. I started off being too charitable. When the fur came in, I gave the trapper an advance. When I sold the fur I tried to give him the balance. It soon became apparent that this system was unworkable. Whose fur had brought what price at a sale months after the fact? Then, fur buying is no simple matter. Grades and quality, size and shape, colour, damages, not to mention market fluctuations, must all be taken into account. Nor was I the only fur buyer anxious to see accounts cleared. If the fur got to Peace River the money stayed there too.

Beaver pelts were a real problem. First, there was the matter of grading which was a matter of gauging size and quality. Size was determined by measuring from between the eyes to the other end and adding the distance across the pelt. Quality was a judgement call involving the fullness of fur and colour. Then there was the matter of damage. Had the hunter used buckshot? Had the beaver spoiled his pelt by rubbing it as he worked under the ice? Had he rubbed off his body fur with his legs as he worked? Had there been a battle resulting in gashes left by vicious teeth?

Nor should we forget government involvement. How could we ever function without government? At that time the beaver pelts were to be stamped. There was no way a forest ranger could be on hand to do this task, so they allowed me to bring my pelts to them at Three Creeks. Once I got there to find no one home, so I tried to leave a message written with the plane's dipstick. I had no pen. Fortunately the demand for stamping was dropped. But there were other complications.

The spring hunt was always looked to as the solver of all financial problems. If during the grubstaking procedure I tried to suggest restraint, I was often reassured that this gun or that pile of traps was no big deal. Was it not just a matter of a beaver blanket or two? Trying to maintain the same degree of optimism in May and June was another matter.

By the time the trappers straggled out of the bush in June, sold me their furs and I got them to the Edmonton Fur Auction, it would be July or even August. Who could get excited about furs in August? The unrealistic prices, which had been dangled before the trapper in the previous fall's fur flyers, bore little resemblance to what I received in August.

There were, however, several redeeming factors. During those first years, there was an abundance of fur. When we drove in to Town early on a Saturday morning we might count 250 rabbits. These allowed a boom in the lynx population. Their price was only a few dollars but was climbing. In later years some pelts sold for $1100.00. Squirrels were abundant. One lot of 6000 just about paid for that beautiful Ambassador straight out of a Toronto showroom. There were also coyote, wolf, marten, fisher and mink pelts as well as tanned moose hides. I never kept records, but I like to think that most of the losses sustained on beaver pelts were offset by gains on winter fur.

During my store's fourth year I let the stock dwindle and the store die. By that time Fleuri L'Hirondelle had set up his trading post nearby. I had no wish to run him competition. Furthermore, the needs of our community were being met and I didn't need the work of running a store.

During earlier days, in the history of that general region, traders like Josie L'Hirondelle and his son Raymond reached out to the outlying trap lines with their trading efforts. One of those outposts was Big Buffalo or Bison Lake. During our time no one traded at Big Buffalo, but the Sawan clan had semipermanent homes there because the settlement was near their trap lines. Several other trappers used that place as a staging spot from where they would journey even farther into the hinterland.

It was a convenience to the trappers to have someone bring trade goods up to Big Buffalo rather than come out themselves. A trip out could easily take a full week. Thus Norman Dafoe and I decided to make a trip up there one weekend. Having agreed to meet Norman at the Cadotte Lake junction on Saturday morning,

I went to Peace River Friday night to get supplies.

We met, as agreed, and set off for points north, I with my heavily loaded Volkswagen, Norman with his Jeep. Incidentally, the carrying capacity of Volkswagens increases greatly as the seats are removed. This little workhorse did acquire an interesting configuration when it was loaded with half a ton of freight or more. The back wheels would assume a knock-kneed stance which became more pronounced with the addition of each hundredweight.

Upon reaching Fish or Haige Lake, we loaded the Jeep and left the Volkswagen. We had gone only a few miles when the Jeep hit a bump, throwing off one of the ten gallon drums of kerosene which we had set on a little platform built on the Jeep's front bumper. A hole was punctured in the oil pan when it hit the drum.

Little Black Sambo was our only option. We trotted back for him, transferred as much of our load from the Jeep as we could, and continued north. We were within a few miles of our destination when we came upon the Joe Sawans stuck with their pick-up in a creek.

When they learned of our supplies they abandoned their plans to take their furs to Peace River, taking them back instead to their cabin. That evening we gathered at Moise's cabin to do some trading. Moise was the patriarch of the Sawan clan. While we were engaged in our dealings, someone went out only to discover that Joe Sawan's cabin was on fire. A cat had knocked over a kerosene lamp. Their whole catch of fur went up in the flames!

What remarkable stoicism those people were capable of! I remember no wringing of hands, nor can I recall the matter ever coming up for later discussion. I regarded the event as a tragedy. They seemed to look on it as one of those things which happen. Moise's grandson, Raymond Sawan, usually known as Blue Eyes, would likely forgive me for including a little incident involving him. I tell it by way of illustrating the ingenuity of our friends.

Raymond had left his vehicle by the trail when he went to his trap line. Upon returning some weeks later, he discovered his

Author, on a visit to Edmonton for a Teachers' Convention, wears a beaded moose-hide jacket made for him by Bella Ominayak as payment for trips to visit her dying father.

battery to be dead. The nearest boost was likely a few days' hike away. What did he do? He took the bar off his chain saw. Replacing it with the V-belt he charged his battery. No problem!

During those years I went off to summer school every summer to polish off a few more courses. Most of these courses involved some pre-session study. Since our trails were impassible during spring and early summer, I was often in the air at least for one trip every day. Fortunately, one could fly till almost midnight. During that same time of the year the spring-hunt fur was coming in. At school I had five grades which I certainly did not plan to slack off on. In other words I was very busy.

One Saturday I became so desperate for a little time that I took my pre-session work with me on a trip to Town, hid behind the old railway station and had a few minutes to myself. Fortunately we were then young and strong.

Chapter 11

Our Family

When I came to my desk this morning to write this chapter, a picture on a church bulletin caught my attention. The photograph pictured three generations giving thanks at a festive table. The person of grandfather was missing, but I suspect his presence was very much among them in the form of a spiritual legacy. Surely one of the smartest things God ever did was to create the family unit.

Luella and I are pleased with our family. So far, a reading of this account could easily convey the impression that my family was unimportant to me. That is hardly the case. Our children can best be brought into this account as I air my philosophy of life regarding child rearing. If struggling parents are thereby helped, I will be glad. As in the case of the Little Buffalo community, I do not wish to overly invade the privacy of the members of our family. The philosophies which I advance are, in a sense, a portrayal of our children and vice versa.

To begin with, I should say that I feel that the creating of a new life is a tremendous responsibility. Thousands of years after Abraham rather casually caused Ishmael to be born, the repercussions still reverberate as guns and fire and bombs explode in the Middle East. On the other hand, Abraham's other bloodline gave us Jesus Christ.

In the same vein, there is not a single bloodline on earth totally bound for Heaven. Am I prepared to accept the fact that, given time, some of my offspring are not going to make Heaven?

Pre-natal influence is very real and very important. This being the case, the thoughtful parent will cause her prenatal activities and attitudes to be determined by the ideals she holds for her offspring.

Child rearing is such an impossible task, parents should realize they are never going to get it right by conniving. What parents are is what they can expect their children to be. Children are not likely to accept a double standard from "moderately good" parents. Children whose parents have made a hash of life often realize that is not the way to operate, and will then set better goals. Their major problem is often lack of teaching and training.

If prenatal influences are of consequence, surely postnatal ones are of tremendous consequence. Some parents seem to feel only the things they will say at some future time need to be guarded. However, their little person is picking up "vibes" from day one. Parents must learn to bite their tongues. They may not then, with their bit tongues, always be the most lively conversationalists, but neither will they have to extinguish wildfires ignited by rude or careless comments.

When people have a choice in the matter, they should choose for their family a setting where the children can have freedom to *be* children without undue supervision. Such freedom allows them to exercise their imaginations, initiatives and judgements. In such a setting they learn to assume responsibility for themselves. Furthermore, a laissez-faire arrangement takes much strain off a mother.

Closely related to this freedom idea is the matter of rules. I was surprised to have one of my fellow teachers suggest that we likely had lots of rules in our home. If we had rules, I fail to recall what they were. Standards, certainly, but there is a vast difference between a standard and a rule. A standard is something for me to live up to partly because I am me and partly because I am part of a family which I support. A rule is an imposition. It was likely someone else's idea. As children live up to standards, they develop self-control and self-respect. When they march to a set of rules, however, they are apt to find the exercise wearisome and burdensome. Tired of control, some throw off the restraint at an early opportunity.

During my third year of teaching there was a family of Walkers in my school. Both parents taught, even though they had a large family. I believe there were seven children. There was something notable about those people. I was never in their home, but I got the sense that there was an unusual bond: not a sentimental oneness, but a unity that issued from family-respect and loyalty. (I believe the legal fraternity honoured one of that family in 1998).

I hoped such an attitude of family loyalty would govern our family. Certainly I didn't desire my children to be arrogant, but I hoped that their attitude would be, "I am an Enns. As a member of that family I will keep from doing certain things. There are other things I will do and be. I will live my life by our family standards."

I never articulated the foregoing for my children, because about the last thing a parent should ever do is compare one child with a sibling, or let it be known that he is expected to behave in a certain fashion because he happens to be a child of a certain professional.

I'm sure the teachers of our children must have wondered at our apparent lack of interest in pushing them. Usually the children's own initiative prompted them to be successful in school. When they were on their own, their initiative and desire to learn remained fresh and lively.

Then there is the matter of the teenager. "Teenager" is a word

Enns children with Evangeline

that is not in my vocabulary. It is far too strong a word to be used casually. The term has too many connotations. Its use often immediately conjures a hodge-podge of unpleasant images. How foolish it is of people to anticipate, often verbally in the presence of their children, with dread, the time when their children will reach a certain stage in their lives! Some seem to feel that their reasonable twelve-year-old will somehow be reborn as a vibrant monster on his thirteenth birthday. Such expectations and fears are most unfortunate and unnecessary!

Prophecies of this nature tend to be self-fulfilling. When the child hears such expectations and fears expressed he is apt to set about living out what is expected of him. He may do this subconsciously but likely with anger. Certainly the wise parent will be aware of natural tendencies in that age group. He will also be keenly cognizant of the fact that there is a host of negative influences about. A positive confidence in youth is tremendously helpful in bringing about a positive result.

When a parent has fearful expectations he is expressing a lack of confidence in his child. If a child loves his parents he is going to desire to please them. If positive expectations exist, in a unified family the young person feels encouraged to make good. This brings me to the most fundamental matter in child rearing.

During the ceremonies opening the 1998 Winter Games at Nagano, Japan, tremendous sophistication was evident. Choirs on five continents joined with an orchestra in Japan to present "An Ode to Joy." The participating groups were in Japan, Germany, South Africa, New York, and Australia. The Japanese participants included the orchestra, a choir and even some of the crowd in the stadium. Japanese electronics wizardry enabled all of the groups to be totally synchronized even though electronic signals do take a few seconds to travel up to satellites and back down to receivers on the other side of our planet. This may have been the first time such levels of technical sophistication had been used in such a vast arena. Peter Mansbridge said even the CBC did not have this technology.

Apart from the equipment, the other reason why such an amazing production could be staged was because all the groups which participated were responding to one conductor. They were all marching to the beat of a single drum, so to speak.

A similar principle can be operative in a family, resulting in the many benefits of unity.

In order to understand the principle, it is necessary to understand spiritual rebirth. A spiritual rebirth involves a turning from the former life to a new life. It involves an act of the will. The convert wills to turn from his own ways, to those of God. During this process he allows his sin account to be paid by the sacrificial payment on his behalf by the death of Christ on Calvary. He acts in faith, fully believing that he is now an accepted member of God's family. In the process he will have received a new heart, to use the usual term. In other words, he will have received a whole new outlook on life—a new set of desires, and standards.

When the members of a family have all experienced such a rebirth and have all received their new "hearts" (attitudes, aspirations, priorities, loves) they can then proceed to march to one drum beat. The result may not be a total utopia. There will always have to be allowance made for individual interpretations and personalities. But serious conflicts will be less likely, for the general intent is now one. This intent does not change during the teen years. Teens can be just as sincere, and perhaps more energetic, about obeying the Divine Drummer as anyone.

Many people react to the suggestion of a rebirth for children with disbelief and skepticism, if not cynicism. I assure my readers that it works. One of our children in particular exhibited a truly noteworthy change of heart from the age of five.

One day his mother discovered him, at an even younger age, lying on his bed contemplating the ceiling. His conclusion was a cynical, "God can't see me through that."

Later on, after he had asked for his new heart, there was a remarkable change in his life. He maintained his strong spirit but his conversion came as a tremendous relief to both his mother, whom he had previously driven to consternation, and his playmate Lyanne, who was then in considerably less danger of receiving a whack to her head with a hammer.

For children, accepting the idea of a cleansed heart is a most natural step. Most have no problem understanding that their

Left to right: Arlyn, Lyndell, Laurella

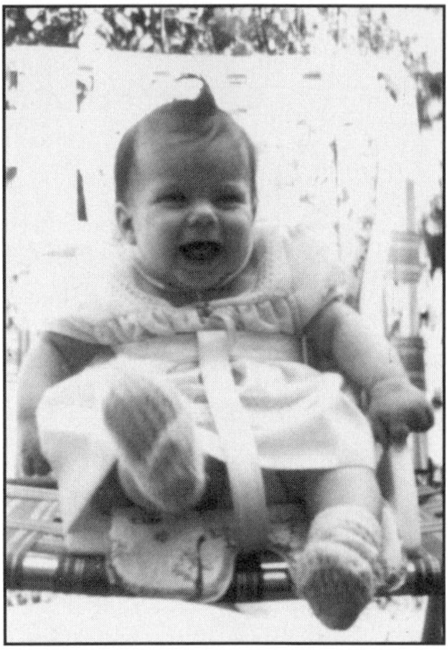

Lanna-Marie
(above & below)

Lyndell

Laurella's first day of school

The children at their grandparents' in Abbotsford

Family with snowpacker used to prepare airstrip

lives are less than perfect. As for accepting the idea of a loving, caring, forgiving God—that's no problem, if they have parents who treat them that way. When children make this decision early they avoid the doubts that often plague adults. The children will become aware of the truth of hellfire as they learn the Scriptures, but the element of fear will not likely enter into a child's conversion experience. Parents need only present the holiness and love of God. The young ones can certainly relate to and accept that.

The matter of punishment must also be clarified. As the number of shot-up bodies and general mayhem increases, people sometimes wonder about the child rearing practices of recent decades.

One of the recent rather tarnished nuggets of modern wisdom is that the rebellious child should be reasoned with, rather than be punished. Let me submit that when people "dialogue" long enough they can make about any activity look, if not totally acceptable, at least reasonable.

When a little person commits a little atrocity and his parent or parent replacement proceeds with a dispassionate discussion of why likely what was done should maybe not have been done, the child draws his own conclusions: "As long as there are no consequences, this can't be a big deal."

On the other hand, if the authority figure shows enough concern to punish the offender, the latter must conclude that the issue at hand must be of some consequence. "Surely this parent who is loving and good to me wouldn't suddenly wish to cause me and himself pain if the matter were not serious."

Reading the foregoing, a person might conclude life for the children was a sombre procedure. I do not think it was. Once parents have such understanding they can then run a quiet, well ordered home in which children go about childhood affairs in contented confidence.

Who was entertaining my children while their parents were busy about their adult affairs? Mostly, they were. We were in the happy position of being able to let them have freedom to play much as they pleased. They had lots of room and company. Their friends included the children both of fellow staff members and of local Aboriginals.

My personal interaction with our own children usually involved other students as well. I always planned to play with the children during recesses. We had simple equipment like giant-strides, teeter-totters, a revolving platform and tether-ball, which served us well. Activities like soccer, soft ball, fox and goose, and skating kept us amused when we were out of doors. Indoors we might play ping-pong or shuffleboard. In the larger schools supervision was regarded as a chore. In the small schools we just assumed it to be part of the day. Rarely did I find playing with the children a chore. Not only did I enjoy the fun with the children but our fun paid big dividends in that it eliminated most discipline problems.

Our shuffleboard was of a home-grown variety—with a difference. Shooting was done with $3^{1/2}$" wooden disks, and all from one end. The counting end resembled a curling house with the "4 foot" circle cut out. A pouch caught the bulls-eye counters.

One recess Danny Sawan entertained us by skipping rope 1500 times. With stamina like that he should have become a great moose hunter, but his days were cut short in a vehicle accident on the Peace River hill.

There were a few family outings. Several come to mind when our children and the Jacksons had good times. Once when Jacksons had a school bus which doubled as a camper, we and the children went toward Bison Lake to an airstrip to picnic and pick berries.

Now there is something about school buses and children that I don't fathom. Given their freedom, children can go on for literally hours, when they are out for field trips and the like, with never a break in their joyous conversation and hubbub. I usually have no idea of what they converse.

In this instance the topic of hilarity involved a series of experiences which seem to have occurred at some railway crossing. This must have been an imaginary one for there wasn't a real one within fifty miles.

Even though the children had their share of fun and games, entertainment for adult members of the Mission was a little thin.

During some of those years, when our staff still included dorm parents, we had at least one form of recreation. After the children were put to bed on Sunday night, the staff would gather at our house for a prayer meeting. I can not speak for the others, but I know that my alertness tended to wane, so that by the time the prayer session was completed I was alert and ready for a little socializing.

Dear old Mr. Ferguson, our pastor, though endowed with the keenest sense of humour, felt it was his duty to show us younger people an example. He would be the first to the door. After he pulled on his boots, he pronounced in his usual droll fashion, "Well, it won't be so funny in the morning."

Nonetheless we younger people, quite unconcerned with the prophecy, the fulfilment of which was both likely and accurate, would gather around the piano for a grand old sing. Mrs. Krause, unhampered by a need for music, would provide the accompaniment with an invigorating gusto. The rest of us would sing, as it seems now, by the hour. No doubt things were less funny in the morning! As for the prophet, he was likely up at 5am milking

Left to right: Rev. Ferguson, Norman Dafoe, Mrs. Krause, Mrs. Thiessen, Luella, Henry

cows and getting proceedings under way.

While the children were little, we were able to have a few pets for them. Possibly the most notable of these was Kona, the Samoyed Husky. There were also cats and horses.

Kona, meaning "snow" in Cree, was a name suggested by one of the Little Buffalo students in response to a naming contest. (prize $1) Kona was a beautiful creature. Her coat was of the finest white wool. Her pretty face was set off and made to appear very alert by a set of pointy ears that stood at attention. She had a gregarious and buoyant personality which caused her to wander. Unfortunately, she succumbed to the temptation to wander once too often. She had taken a shine to rabbits in snares. People needed them for food, but they didn't need Kona.

One incident involving a cat, was particularly amusing. One of our kittens was to be launched into a career of motherhood but obviously no one had revealed to her the pertinent facts of life. Her time of deliverance came as an utter shock to her as she one day reclined on the front step. Registering a most obvious total surprise, she dashed around the house to the back step. The pains went with her, so back to the front step she tore. How many such trips were involved in the delivery, I'm not certain. In time, the process nonetheless proved successful.

One of our horses was a Shetland pony. She would jar loose the teeth of anyone who would ride her but she could give a better ride when pulling a light little cart which Graydon Dennis made. The wheels were from a motorcycle, the frame of 3/4" pipe. The cart made for a pleasant jaunt and there was no shortage of space for driving.

By the time we had spent a school year in the bush at Little Buffalo, we felt that we owed our family a change. Summer school usually precluded a lot of freedom, but still allowed us to take our children to see their grandparents and other relatives.

One Easter train trip took us from Edmonton to Abbotsford, B.C. We often smile as we remember that one. Laurella was then learning to take her place in the world. She was a cute little lady who often attracted attention. Several ladies wished to be nice, so by way of making conversation they wondered what her name was. Both they and we were amused to discover it was

"Mith Ennth." Mother and Dad were always referred to as Mr. or Mrs.; so why not share the glory?

On the homeward trip we shared the coach with a fellow who broke his frequent naps into segments with sustained swigs from a brown bag. Having refreshed himself, he would doze off again only to come partly awake with a resounding and sustained, "Ahh—ha"! Witnessing this performance repeatedly, Laurella thought she should try it on for size. Her rendition lacked some of the fellow's resounding resonance but it was nonetheless, a rather impressive effort by our little "Mith Ennth."

One summer our family tent-trailered to the east coast of Canada. By that time my Bachelor of Education degree seemed within reach, so we felt that a break in the summer school routine might be justified. Twelve almost consecutive summers at university did seem like quite a stretch. During that trip we saw and experienced what one would expect in a cross country journey. I had to marvel that the voyageurs could have travelled such distances by canoe.

During another summer we flew commercially to Montreal for Expo. The most remarkable aspect of that trip was that we nearly got to ride a bus home along with a family's worth of children. I tried to confirm our flight from the Expo site, but calling the airlines from there was not easy. As everywhere else, a person had to wait in line. When I finally reached the telephone, the number was busy. Back to the end of the line—by the time I got through to the airlines people, our seats had been given to others. Fortunately, some dear soul repented of her ways and gave us back our seats. What a bus ride that would have been!

In all, I feel our time at Little Buffalo was enriching. What we lacked in elaborate facilities we made up for with freedom. There are no substitutes for freedom! If sometimes there did appear to be an abundance of work, that was fine too. Fortunately, work is usually all the recreation I need. I do remember forcing myself to stay at my desk preparing for summer school. Others were outside playing ball and I would have preferred to join them. That sort of longing was rare, however. My normal mind set was to be happy with another task completed.

Chapter 12

To Hunt a Moose or Catch a Fish

In the Little Buffalo environment the perception of a man's manliness lay largely in how many moose he could kill. A common taunt among the youngsters regarding an awkward person was, "He'll never be a moose hunter!" Arlyn, growing up with the native children, was once heard to say, "I wish Daddy would shoot something." All his friends had stories to relate of fathers who shot moose. He had few such stories, but his friends were sympathetic.

I did like to go moose hunting with some of the local men. Time was a problem, but with the quality of guiding I enjoyed, a person could be almost certain of a kill if we left Friday after school and returned Saturday evening. One hunt stands out.

The September 8th arrived when I was supposed to join Peter Sawan at Bison Lake for a moose hunt. At 3:30^{pm}, I lost little time flying the route indicated by such familiar landmarks as Marten, Otter, Fish and finally Bison Lakes. Lakes were our signposts. Peter had preceded me by road and was waiting at Bison Lake. He hopped in with me and we carried on to Bison Lake fire tower.

What we beheld there was surely a moose hunter's dream. (Later when we walked about I was amazed to see not moose tracks, but trails. The area might have been a cow pasture.) While circling the strip, before landing, we spotted three moose close at hand. Upon landing we started down the strip on foot. This was another of those cases when, before I realized that there was a moose at hand, he was "dead meat." Having attended to this fellow in a most preliminary fashion we set out to look for one of those others which we had spotted from the air. Darkness descended quickly upon us so we returned to our young bull and the plane.

That was the end of the fun part. Soon the weather began to turn miserable. We had a few blankets and planned to sleep under the stars. But there were none, just rain and discomfort. During the night we moved indoors. We removed the three seat cushions from the plane and made a kind of bed on the uneven cabin floor. Daylight, such as it was, finally came. Things looked very bleak so we decided to make a dash for Peter's home at Bison.

This was not a long flight, about 15 miles, but chancy under the circumstances. There was no thought of taking much meat with us. Back at Bison, it was good to be taken in by Peter's parents who also lived there. This was sort of a headquarters for the Sawan clan. We waited through Saturday but the weather did not improve. Sunday also brought no relief. Monday was another miserable day, unfit for flying. That Monday was one of the very few days in my teaching career when I failed to be in my classroom.

Toward Monday evening, flight seemed possible. I bid my kind hosts farewell and set off toward the south and home. About the time I was going by Otter Lakes the scenery below

Right to left: Great White Hunter, Guide Peter Sawan and his two sons.

began to look very strange. All I could conclude was that a terrific storm must have hit. Trees were in a terrible state of disarray. Trunks were bent seemingly double. The bush was a mess.

Upon my arrival home the story unfolded. There had been a great, wet snowfall. Being early in September, the poplars had not yet lost their leaves. Thus, as the heavy snow clung to the leaves, the accumulation weighted the trees, doubling them over into a snarled jumble difficult to imagine. Evergreens are designed for that sort of thing—poplars are not.

The first matter to be attended to during those first several days at home was a “bug” which I had acquired during my excursion. By the following Saturday I was sufficiently recovered to try to retrieve my meat. By that time the weather was fine but upon landing, a problem became apparent. The strip had been thoroughly soaked. Likely the same snowfall which hit farther south had dumped on the tower strip.

Take-off was going to be problematic, so I loaded only 125 pounds of meat and took off for Peace River where it was to be processed. On my next trip I became aware of how fortunate I had been to get off. On the strip was a large chunk of mud which had collected on the tail wheel. It must have fallen off at a most opportune time allowing me to get away.

The following week the weather was fine. A recovery of the remaining meat seemed possible and advisable. But I was too late; by that time there was nothing to recover. Likely some bear had felt he needed a bedtime snack and had helped himself. He left not a bit of evidence. Previously I had hung the meat in the trees. It was all gone, as was everything else—horns, hide, entrails, the lot—no half measures there!

Other hunts come to mind. Once I joined my brother, Dr. P.S. Enns, for a hunt with Peter Sawan. We got a moose as per plan, but what I remember most vividly was a remarkable production put on by a beaver and several of his concubines. The object of their attention was a substantial tree leaning over their pond. They must have figured this fellow was oversized at the base so they chewed out steps—Pete remembers five or six—up the leaning trunk, making a staircase of a human carpenter’s specifications. When they reached the proper height they chopped off the tree, dropping it into their pond.

Another time I was out with Harvey Whitehead and his dad. I learned something about saving labour on that trip. Instead of clearing deadfalls from our wagon route they would simply lay two smaller pieces on either side of the fallen tree making a ramp which would allow the wagon to pass. Later that evening I received a lesson in quietness and patience. Harvey, in preparation for listening for moose, wrapped himself in a blanket, mounted a mound left by a crawler, and became a statue. I had no idea that anyone could stand so still so long.

What happened the following morning was astounding. We had broken camp and were prepared to continue down the cutline with the team and wagon. Before we got under way someone spotted a moose coming toward us, slowly and steadily, down the cutline. As we hid in the bush that beautiful young bull kept coming. When he was within easy range he paused, turned broadside and began to nibble at some foliage. He presented a perfect target. One felt almost a bit guilty for taking advantage of him in his vulnerability.

One of the favourite methods of hunting moose during the rutting season is to call them. The hunter prepares a birch-bark bugle which he then uses to produce moose-type noises. I had never witnessed one being used in real life but was prepared to give the method a try. There was a certain element of risk involved, for moose do not appreciate human involvement in their private affairs. Albert Laboucan could testify to that.

He had shot a bull, breaking its foreleg. The bull was understandably resentful and proceeded to make Albert aware of his sentiments. Albert made himself scarce under a brush pile. The bull climbed over that pile with his stump serving as a leg. Albert lived to tell the story; as for the moose, I don't believe I heard.

My moose-calling session requires a trip both forward and backward in time. We, by the time of that hunt, were living at LaCrete several hundred miles north of Little Buffalo. When I flew between the two settlements I would see an airstrip south of the Buffalo Head Hills. Upon closer inspection it seemed there were two features about that strip that would make it a highly desirable hunting spot. There was a shack for shelter, and, what looked from the air to be a salt-lick.

Having taken note of the position of the strip I decided to investigate one Sunday afternoon. Now when you fly you can see a lot, but you cannot see everything. For instance, you cannot see saplings growing on an abandoned airstrip. Thus, when in my happy innocence I landed, my awareness of reality received a major jolt. The saplings, which I had not detected from the air, made an awful ruckus on the metal fuselage and stopped their noise only when the plane ended its roll.

Now it is one thing to land in a situation like that but it is another to take off! When you land you can avoid some obstructions by keeping the tail down and the prop out of the rubbish. When you take off you want that prop down and the tail up for the take off run; but that way there is the problem of hitting things with the propeller. This is not an eminently healthy situation—neither for props nor mortals.

I carried a hatchet with me, if not much else in the line of emergency equipment. Space was always at a premium. This hatchet I wielded with zeal. The growth was fairly thick and Cessna 140's do not get off in 50 yards.

If I was going to do all that work, I reasoned that I might just as well plan to come back to use my newly fashioned strip. Finding the cleared section from the air was going to be a problem unless I could somehow mark it. Resources were limited, but I was wearing a white undershirt which produced a fairly decent supply of ribbons. These I strung out in two rows to mark the proposed landing zone.

Takeoff Sunday was not marred by the clatter which had accompanied the landing; a return trip seemed within reason.

I believe I returned on a Friday night, spent the night and was ready to take my moose on Saturday. Gun and horn in hand, I made my way to a judicious position well up the strip. Having given my horn a mighty squawk, I listened. Sure enough, a moose responded and started to come! I couldn't believe what I had done was all that was required, so I sounded off the second time. That was my mistake. He detected the lack of authenticity and took off, crashing through the bush. The moral of this story would indicate, “Contain your zeal,” or better still, ”Get a guide.”

I went fishing a few times. Just beyond Marten River lay Joker Lake. It was not a large body of water but one of the few lakes of that area with fish. One day I hopped over there, landed on the ice, chopped a hole and started pulling out fish. Even though the three largest jacks made off with my spoons, I still had two dozen tasty pickerels and northern jackfish left after only an hour’s effort.

An added benefit of this trip was that I knew where to land when I was later asked to transport an apparently sick child to hospital from a nearby trapper’s cabin. When on skis, I always breathed a little easier landing on a lake which I had previously visited. Hidden overflow was always a consideration, as were cracks, hard drifts, and pressure ridges.

Chapter 13

A Green Hill Far Away

While we are on the topic of recreation, another trip comes to mind. This session transpired one beautiful Sunday afternoon in March, 1965. I didn't often fly for fun but that day after church, I got the urge. Laurella was the only child who wanted to go with me. The day was warm so the plane started without hesitation. Takeoff was no problem, because the strip had been well rolled with our rubber-tired packer.

When we flew over our little lake it appeared inviting. Snow covered the lake with a soft, unruffled blanket. Against my better judgement, I succumbed to the temptation to just touch-and-go. I knew better than to land because we had great volumes of snow that winter. So I did the right things—carburetor heat on, throttle back, attitude right—but there was one little detail I had overlooked. As I idled in on my approach the motor cooled. When the skis touched and I needed full power, instead of the healthy roar that I needed, we got a pop-pop. Too late did we gain full power. Because of that momentary hesitation, the snow caught us and we were down. Anything I could do after that was an exercise in futility.

I started off by tramping a circle around each ski so I could swing the tail around. Then I tried to follow my tracks in an effort to take off. This was a totally hopeless gesture of desperation. I was going to have to come up with something a lot smarter than that.

The first problem was to get our bodies off the lake. I asked Laurella if she would wait for me as I went for help. She was, understandably, afraid to be left alone out there in the middle of the lake. I was going to have to carry her, but how? The snow was easily to my waist and very soft. Snowshoes were what I needed but did not have, so I was going to have to improvise. The seat cushions offered hope. Tearing a towel, which I normally used to wipe condensation off the windscreen, into strips, I made a rope to loop around each cushion. When I put my feet under the ropes I could stand on the cushions and shuffle along. With Laurella on my back, we set off. She was inclined to choke me as she hung on, so I looped my necktie through my belt so she could hang on to that.

We struggled on. After each spill into those depths of snow, we would sort ourselves out and try once more. Laurella must have found the process somewhat boring, for as we faltered onward she had a suggestion, "Daddy, why don't you sing 'There is a Green Hill Far Away?'" That was a current favourite with the children. I had to admit the suggestion was suitable. I was less certain of its timeliness. When we got to the trail which skirted the lake, Bill Askin was there with his dogs to take us home.

We had solved problem A. Problem B remained. The matter of the plane needed attention. There was some urgency in this for during the up-coming Easter break I was to have the terigia removed from my eyes. This operation was to transpire in Edmonton. Who knew what or if I would be able to see after that? Time was not on my side, since the spring thaws were coming.

Today an operation of that nature is not a great matter. About ten years later I had one removed again. The specialist attended to the matter in his office while I watched. He just peeled the skin-like growth away and sent me off down the street. I could not believe what was happening, but there was no need for anything more. I was fine.

In 1965, an operation of that nature was a substantial undertaking. There were two trips to the operating room, one on Friday and another on Monday. After a week of convalescence in the hospital I went home and remained in the house for days. When I did go back to school I pulled the shades most of the way down and covered the lower parts of the windows with white paper. Even then I could hardly endure the light. Furthermore, my depth perception was poor and I had to go through several changes of glasses before my eyes settled down. Of course, I had no idea all this would transpire, but I knew the plane had to come off the lake. Enter Charlie!

Luella was cooking for the dorm children that year. To give her a break I would get up on Sunday mornings to give the children their breakfast. On that particular morning, as I was upstairs above the dining room getting the cereal, I looked out the window to see Charlie. Now Charlie was our old black horse whose lot in life had on varied occasions involved bailing out his more frail human counterparts. At this time he had checked in to see if there might not be a handout offered during a tough winter. That morning his presence had not been of great significance.

As I considered what to do about my plane, Charlie came to mind. A plan was beginning to jell. The dorm boys were usually ready for some activity, especially on a quiet Sunday afternoon, so I asked them to find Charlie. He hadn't wandered far, so they brought him home.

Monday after school I harnessed him, connected him to a six foot log, and set off for the plane. This time it was my turn to ride. Charlie, of course, felt persecuted, having to wade through

Marilyn Krause on Charlie, the horse which helped me get the plane off the lake

all that snow, but the cause was worthy. When we arrived at the plane I re-hitched Charlie, causing him to pull the log at right angles to himself. With this contrivance we disturbed the snow. Tuesday we repeated the procedure. (Here one must understand that when snow falls and lies undisturbed it can lie for indefinite periods without ever losing its fluff and insulating powers. Once it is disturbed, however, either by wind or human activity, it freezes and can become hard to a point where a heel can hardly leave a mark.)

By Wednesday I expected my new airstrip to be useable. With a borrowed pair of snowshoes I made my way to the plane. The weather was warm enough that starting the plane was no problem. Between Charlie's good work and the low fuel tanks, I was able to get off with no problem.

(On a later low level approach over deep snow I remained somewhat more aloof. Roy Alm's crawler had acquired an ailment while clearing land for the co-op. Parts were required out in the bush. When I picked them up at the airport, I tied them to a rip cord. Later, when I approached the drop site, I hung them

Jimmy Ominayak's two horsepower schoolbus, with school in background

out the door so that I could attend to the approach. When I got near the Cat, down there in the deep snow, I had only to pull the slipknot.) Not all bombing runs end on such a happy note. Roy was happy to get his parts; the co-op work could happily progress; and I could go to my classroom, having done my little chore.

Considering such matters, one must conclude that the boundary between work and recreation is not well defined. Likely the finer the line, and the more blurred, the happier the individual. I suppose one of the reasons why recreation is so important to many people is because they are not wholly satisfied with their workaday life. Surely the happiest situation must be one in which the work of each day is a joy. Then a person does not have to add recreation to his schedule because his necessary work is his recreation. How can one improve on happiness? "Find a job that you enjoy; and you will never have to work a day in your life!" Does it really matter a lot whether one is hunting moose, fishing, flying a plane, or teaching a class of children, if he is content?

Typical trapline transportation in Little Buffalo

Chapter 14

We Wind Down the Boarding Activities

From the outset, people involved in the boarding situation had reservations. There were certain pluses in the system, to be sure. For example, one year when only some of the students lived at home, we had 99% attendance for five months of the year. There may have been a few children on the trapline. In a quiet, ordered situation of that nature, the children can really progress. But there's a downside in separating children from their families. As time went on, various developments, events and considerations pointed to a termination of the boarding endeavours.

We eventually did not have to concern ourselves any longer about boarding children from Marten River. That settlement had been found by the prevailing outside political/religious powers to be inconvenient in a pristine wilderness so the people were 'persuaded' to move to Cadotte Lake. To insure that they would not return, their cabins were bulldozed. I do not believe the people thus uprooted ever recovered any degree of independence.

A school had been built at Cadotte Lake. Most families, by that time, had cabins near Little Buffalo or Cadotte. Staffing for the dorms was difficult to find. The deciding blow came when one of our major buildings was reduced to ashes. It housed our large laundry machine, the power plant, our tools; and served as a warm garage for the tractor and a truck. Rebuilding seemed out of the question. The time was right to terminate the boarding arrangement.

By then Mr. Ferguson had brought along a fine little herd of cattle which, in the light of the current developments, were no longer needed. The dispersal of the herd became my responsibility. During the Easter break of 1968 I volunteered to haul a load of young animals to Edmonton to be sold.

Our 1950 three-quarter ton International had the conventional box replaced by a wooden one with a stock-rack. This box was about seven feet by ten feet. The wheels were covered with plank wells. Having loaded all the animals we wanted to ship, we found that the squeeze was too tight, but I was prepared to make the effort regardless.

Problems weren't long in developing. Soon one of the animals was down and there seemed no way of getting it up because of the tightness of the fit. Furthermore, they broke through the plank over one wheel; as they milled around they would step on the wheel. I certainly didn't want to lose one of Mr. Ferguson's precious animals or break legs either. Stopping by the roadside, I eased the congestion by off-loading one of the steers. Even though I could now get the downed animal up, there was no way to reload the one on the road. Using a chain in the truck, I tied it to a tree beside the trail. This trip was not to be. Obviously, I could not leave that animal tied indefinitely to the tree so I returned the bulk of the load to the Mission and recovered the tethered animal the next day.

Later these, as well as most of the other animals, were transported to market with more adequate equipment and with greater success.

For some reason we held back one big red milk cow even after the departure of Mr. Ferguson. Perhaps the departure of *all* the animals seem too traumatic, and that cow eased the loss.

By that time only Mildred Mallinger and our family remained on the yard. Keeping the cow was not a smart idea. The winter of 68–69 was cold—really cold. Surely it was the coldest winter I have experienced. As I remember things, the temperature dropped to –40° Fahrenheit on December 18 and hovered between that and –63° until February 8. It was cold!

If a person has never endured –60° degrees, he has an experience yet to discover. Minus forty is cold—few would differ with that opinion—but with some care and caution the temperature need not be dangerous. Minus sixty is, to put the matter very simply, dangerous. Upon first stepping outdoors, the danger isn't immediately apparent, partly because of the deadness of the air. This fact is in itself a problem because it tends to promote casualness. Certainly, fresh air never seems fresher, even pleasant. But before long the cold pierces anything you might be wearing and when it does, "piercing" is the correct word. At –40° you can double your fingers in your mitts and by other measures gain relief. At –60° relief is difficult to obtain. Once the cold has penetrated, it's there! You don't play games with temperatures of –60°.

During one of thosc –63° degree mornings, Mildred Mallinger —a soldier of the first order—and I, were returning from a teachers' convention in Edmonton. We were getting on quite well until one of our front tires on the International sprang a leak. Fortunately we were able to substitute a spare and get rolling again. Meanwhile, back home, Luella was having her own problems.

Because of the extreme cold, the oil refused to run from the outside tank to the furnace—despite the fact that it was winter diesel.

The propane for the cookstove had stopped vaporizing. The situation in the house was getting set to become unpleasant!

Norman Dafoe aboard Omego, horse of the unauthorized furlough

Luella had the children stay in bed as long as possible. She was planning to take them to Calahesins' to keep them warm at their wood heater. The measure proved unnecessary because, after the sun shone on the fuel tank, the oil began flowing again.

It was my lot to milk old Red that winter. She spent most of her time at the straw stack, but I brought her into the barn for milking. Somewhere I heard of a farmer who under similar circumstances claims to have dispensed with his milk pail choosing rather to take the frozen product to the house in coils. Likely the story is somewhat overstated. I continued to use the pail, finding that system superior to the coil method.

In time, all the cattle were sold and the money put into a parsonage. That building was later hauled down to Lac La Biche where it now serves as a men's dorm at the Key Way Tin Bible School. During the time this parsonage remained at Little Buffalo it served as the home for Billy and Shirley Jackson as well as Raymond and Janice Sparklingeyes and their children. Both Billy and Raymond were Cree speaking ministers whom we much appreciated having available to our community.

As I mention that house I am reminded of how it and several other buildings were serviced with running water from the central pressure system located in the plant house. If backhoes existed in those days their services were not available to us. We wanted to pipe water to the various buildings from the pressure system. Trenching those distances by hand was a huge task so it was decided we would use a different method.

At intervals, we dug holes that were about two feet wide, eight feet deep, and six or eight feet long. Using four foot lengths of $1^{1/2}$" steel pipe, we would aim carefully at the next hole, shove a length in with a hydraulic jack, fasten a second length, push that one in and continue thus until the first lengths emerged, hopefully in the next hole. Then a plastic line was fastened to the last length of pipe and the process repeated in reverse, this time with a pull. As the lengths of pipe were pulled through, they brought with them the plastic line. At the next hole the process was repeated. Though the process was in the end successful it was a slow procedure, necessitating leaving the holes open for a longer period of time.

One Saturday, helpers who had come from Peace River to work for the day were preparing to leave. Mildred Mallinger, ever one to keep in contact by letter, had prepared some mail she was going to send with our departing friends. In her haste, and in the prevailing darkness, she had forgotten about the holes. Dashing along unsuspectingly, she crash-landed in one of our pushing holes. How she managed to fall that distance without injury, I have no idea. I believe it was her good friend, Arlyn, who discovered her plight. His great sympathy may not have been accurately reflected by his innocent inquiry, "What are you doing down there?" But I'm certain she appreciated any condolences forthcoming at that time!

During the time our activities were in progress at Little Buffalo, different people reached out into Marten River and Cadotte Lake with an effort to take them news from the Bible. During my time both George Dunn, and later Norman Dafoe, visited these communities on Sundays. In later years I would go to Cadotte Lake. Marten River by then had ceased to exist.

In my mind, the efforts of both George and Norman are linked to the horse Omego, which first George and then Norman used for transportation. Now, Omego was a horse "of a different colour," as they say. One can merely surmise what manner of "cauldron of adversity" was instrumental in shaping his rigorous personality. As to appearance, if he wasn't a quarterhorse he nonetheless looked the part. He was a fine animal, if the observer closed his eyes to certain eccentricities.

When functioning on his own terms, Omego performed with alacrity, but it seems he found missionary service wearisome. At one juncture he assumed for himself the right of a furlough. His arrangements were to the point and effective.

The inspiration came to Omego on a Sunday, while transporting George either to or from Marten River. His innovative approach to the situation was to scrape George off in the bush and transport himself to points unknown. Those points remained unknown for a month even though George searched for his lost steed, and made inquiries.

When Omego was finally discovered, he had lost his bridle, but was still wearing the saddle. Even in that matter his disdain for convention was quite apparent. Most horses settle for wearing their saddles on the top side. Omego chose to wear his on his underside.

My own experiences with Omego were rare, brief and dramatic. Every several years I like to ride a horse. One such urge came to me when Omego was available. Our jaunt was to be a brief one within the confines of the school yard. Omego must have regarded this activity as frivolous, unworthy of one such as he. Suddenly he dashed for the bluff of trees growing near the north end of the yard. (Maybe he felt furlough time had again arrived.) It was only with a particularly dedicated effort that I persuaded him to alter course.

In time, Omego's ownership passed into the hands of Norman and Tilda Dafoe who had by then moved to Newbrook. Omego was to hitch a ride to his new assignment. The loading procedure offered further insights into the horse's unique personality.

Enter Tom Castle and Dorothy Bott: these young people came to us as an engaged couple in order to give us some short-term assistance. The time for their union arrived so I fetched us a preacher from Peace River.

The formalities completed, and their period of service over, the time for a honeymoon had arrived. Some people set off with cans rattling but, in lieu of cans, we proposed to send Omego with them. In that sort of setting you make every trip count. There was a problem, however; Omego was having difficulties being reconciled with the idea of a move. At seven o'clock one morning we started trying to get him into that famous International. We battled and fought for hours. Finally we got him up and in but he wasn't done yet. Up and over the side of that $5^{1/2'}$ box he went, landing on his back with an awful thump! The blow must have taken the wind not only out of his lungs but also his sails.

Getting him up the second time must have taken less than an hour because by 10 o'clock he was reloaded and gone. Likely the Castles are telling the story to their grandkids by now. Not everyone gets to begin a honeymoon with the likes of Omego!

In later years, with Omego gone, I was compelled to resort to car, tractor, or plane travel when I visited Cadotte. When I did,

Danny and Mary Calahesin

Mildred Mallinger and Luella conducted Sunday School at Little Buffalo in the mornings. Then we had a service in the evening. When we moved on, the Allen Sharps followed us and took on that part of the work.

Chapter 15

Characters Whose Memories We Cherish

As Luella and I sift through a great collection of memories, one of the elements of our lives that we marvel at is the quality of the people with whom we have been associated over the years and in various places. Numerous characters emerge out of the haze that stretches back over the years.

Some of these people were fellow teachers. (We have a special regard for our Maritime friends.) Some were ordinary community members. Others were various professionals serving in capacities other than teaching. Then there were the missionaries. Likely none of our friends have had tougher rows to hoe than the missionaries, yet with no others have we celebrated more joy-

Rev. J. F. Ferguson (now interred in the Wetaskiwin area)

ously. The special circumstances which people in isolated places share seem to forge strong links.

The question that comes to mind is: "Are people everywhere so fine or have we been particularly fortunate?" Many are deserving of comment. I will commemorate a few, even if only briefly.

Danny and Mary Calahesin lived next to the Mission at Little Buffalo. They were our seniors by about 40 years. Because they were markedly more senior than we, but had never had a family of their own, they preferred to think of us as their grandchildren. They liked us to call them 'Kohkam' (grandmother) and 'Mosoom' (grandfather). They were a frugal, hard-working and well-off couple. Danny trapped well into his eighties and maybe even nineties, while Mary skinned the animals. In earlier years they used to haul freight, each with a wagon, between Lesser Slave Lake and Peace River. They had also raised cattle, Mary again working along with Danny.

They were hardly what one would call vain, but Mary did allow herself one small vanity. Both were always very aware of local affairs, but Mary was the spokesperson. Some events impressed her less than others, which fact elicited a rather frequently reiterated reappraisal of their own married status. As each anniversary or decade rolled past, her observation would be "Forty (or maybe fifty, or sixty) years married and never separate." The number would vary but the second part, never.

I still smile remembering the time that Danny's horses disappeared. I agreed to take him up to look around to see if we could spot them. Likely he had never been in a plane. When I had taxied out to the strip to meet him, I saw him approaching from his church which was on their side of the airstrip. I guessed that he had felt that his saints should be alerted to the occasion of his airplane ride. At least Danny was much easier to keep aloft than Harry Lambert (the fur trader of the shoot-out) had been. Harry also wanted to check for horses, so we went up to look around. Harry was a big, heavy man better designed to be hauled in a pick-up truck than in a little Cessna 140. Furthermore, I had not had a chance to run the motor in properly after the overheating incident, so I wanted to keep the revs down, but with that kind of weight to keep above the trees, there was little choice.

Joe Noskey would never have imagined himself as being history book material. Likely that is part of the reason why it is my pleasure to mention him. Joe's English didn't amount to much, but we somehow managed to communicate in an elementary fashion.

I like to remember Joe because he was one of the hardy old-timers who, through old fashioned work and effort, managed to retain his independence through most of his years. His trap line lay some four days journey east of Bison Lake. Usually he travelled by dog team. When he got to his trap line there was not a great deal of comfort. He never felt a need to construct line cabins; he would simply sleep outside at whatever the temperature.

When pension time arrived, Joe had a problem because no one had made a note of his original arrival, many years previous. Lunch time occurred during the time the judge was hearing his case, so judge, Joe, and interpreter, Billy Jackson among others, left the court room together. As they were going down the stairs the judge wondered about Joe's beat up hand. When the interpreter asked Joe his response was, "Oh, the judge wouldn't understand. He wouldn't know about muzzle-loaders." Actually, the judge did understand. His response was, "Well, if he's old enough to have used that kind of gun, he's old enough for a pension."

Another former associate whom we remember with love and respect was our Reverend Joseph Ferguson. Yes, we remember him as a minister, but we remember him even more distinctly as a person who was characterized by self-discipline, hard work, faithfulness and a great sense of humour.

When my passenger, Peter Sawan, had to guide the plane into the yard because we had lost our brakes on one of those Big Buffalo trips, Mr. Ferguson wondered aloud, "Did he make you get out often to push?"

An earlier incident is also illustrative. Mr. Ferguson moved into the log cabin which we had occupied when we first arrived. It seems that one day as he was preparing meat and potatoes on the woodstove for dinner, things got somewhat out of hand. When the smoke had drifted away and Mr. Ferguson was sorting through the ashes of his cabin he discovered the potatoes which he had been cooking. His observation was, "Well now, if I could find my roast, I could have my dinner!"

"Good night!" was as close to profanity as Mr. Ferguson ever came. When our large multi-purpose garage was burning, some of the children ran to alert the old gentleman. Upon hearing of this calamity his reaction was, "Good night!" The children chuckled about that one, no doubt wondering about the goodness of a night during which our garage was going up in flames.

Mr. Ferguson came to us as an old gentleman. He had served his time as a pastor. At an age when most people have long since retired he still had a real desire to serve. His wife had passed away before we got to know him. Not only did he preach faithfully, but he did about anything else that needed doing as other staff came and went. He would look after the cattle—and he was a good cattleman—supervise the boys in the dorm, help in the kitchen, anything.

On one occasion, only Mr. Ferguson and Luella were left at the Mission. I believe Delores Dunn was awaiting a baby in Town. George and I had gone in the previous evening to see her. We were driving the Power Wagon, but because the trail was "iffy" we took the scenic detour through Marten River. This route added to the length of the trip so, even though we spent most of the night on the trail, I was late for school the next morning. When Mr. Ferguson discovered that only he and Luella were left, his comment was, "Well, it looks like we're the only two men left on the place." Luella took her class, as usual, and Mr. Ferguson took mine. When I arrived at about ten o'clock, his comment was, "I've done about everything else on the place, I thought I might just as well teach too."

Remembering what a fine old soldier he was makes the unfortunate circumstances of his demise seem even sadder. I have rarely repeated the circumstances of his death, but I will do so here out of respect and in honour of his memory.

When we left for summer school at Grouard during the summer of 1967, only Mr. Ferguson and Harry Forest were left. At this point I must explain about our plumbing. Earlier the account of our water system was given. That solved the "in" problem.

Mildred Mallinger

There remained the "out" problem. Canadian Propane seemed to have the answer. They were selling what was really an incinerator. Instead of flushing the toilet you simply closed the lid. This triggered a mini explosion and a mighty roar of flame and fan. The results were a few ashes and a truly sensational smell in the yard, if there happened to be a down draft.

By the time our family wanted to leave for the summer this toilet no longer functioned so I removed it from the house and took it to Town for repairs. With the toilet went the shut-off valve. I used the valve on the large tank outside to stop the flow of propane. Because no one was going to be using our house while we were gone, this procedure seemed safe enough.

Since the powerplant ran only when lights were needed or when chores like ironing or washing needed to be done, our source of refrigeration was the propane fridge. During the summer, for some reason the fridge at the dining hall ceased to function, so Mr. Ferguson decided to use the one at our house. Being unaware of the open line, he opened the valve at the tank.

When he went to light the pilot light on the fridge, disaster struck. Community members came to help him and Harry fight the blaze. They managed to save the house but the effort of running with heavy pails of water was too much for Rev. Ferguson. He died right there of a heart attack.

In his memory I would say, "Thank you Mr. Ferguson for being such a faithful friend and soldier. We cherish your memory!"

Harry took the body to Town in the old International. One could feel that the old warrior deserved better than to be subjected to such an indignity. Yet this matter, as all others, where this old saint is concerned, will be weighed, judged and rewarded in a timely and appropriate fashion.

Rev. Ferguson was buried near his former home in central Alberta.

Only later did Luella and I learn of this tragedy.

There is a brief sequel to this account that I should like to include before I go on to our next character.

The explosion and fire produced by the propane leak caused considerable damage to the contents of the storeroom in which the toilet appliance had been located. Among the casualties were my beautiful .308 rifle, Luella's wedding dress and many of our pictures including movies which we had taken over the years. Fortunately the movies, which included most of our baby pictures, were not totally destroyed.

Repairs to the house were required but the new school year was already under way before they were undertaken. When the repair crew came out they were loaded for bear. The repairmen were going to board themselves in the school so they brought their own supplies. Even though the repairs required were relatively minor, the fellows must have planned to stay two weeks, judging by the piles of food.

These carpenters were like various others of our visitors. Before more than a few days had passed they were ready to climb walls. They worked as hard and as long as possible, completing the work in short order. Having done their work they could not wait for a truck to come in to rescue them and their gear. Thus I was commissioned to fly in to Peace River to charter a larger plane. This plane made two trips for them and what couldn't be loaded was left. I still have some mementos.

To those of us living in that isolation the reaction of such people was interesting. They seemed to be afflicted with a type of claustrophobia. We never felt that way.

Mildred Mallinger was another of that cadre of old soldiers who contributed her fair share and more. Even in her late years she was petite. She was the sort of person who had obviously learned to control her natural impulses, and seemed quite capable of living in the shadows until a need to assert herself arose. Then she could come forward and do what needed doing and be quite vocal about it too.

Our children referred to her as "Bano." She must have been okay because Lyndell, who always had a good eye for the finer things of life, at one early juncture announced that he was going to marry Bano.

Mildred had taught at Little Buffalo on two different occasions prior to our arrival. She came back for a third session which coincided with our last years there. She continued teaching after we left.

Mildred had a special affinity for the children of the hinterland. Not only did she appear at Little Buffalo three times, but I was interested, during my recent reading of a book about Dr. Jackson, *The Homemade Brass Plate,* to be reminded that she also taught at Keg River Post. Muskeg River was also included in her teaching itinerary as were several other northern schools.

Death came to her, too, while she was still in the harness. She and others were supervising their classes on a field trip to Jasper. (She was very good at that sort of thing, as well as being a fine teacher). One morning, as she was beginning her day, she had a massive stroke. Had she had her wish in the matter I am satisfied that she would have chosen to go as she did—while still involved with her dear children.

The following is one of those accounts which one relates with hesitancy out of respect for the memory of the deceased. If, however, it is not related, the very memory will cease to exist.

It seems less than proper that someone like our former student, Josephine, should live, die and be thoroughly forgotten! Furthermore, while we seek to preserve the privacy of our friends, there is a danger of promoting the lie—so often perpetrated by anthropologists, and all their cousins—that all is joy, light and peace among those less touched by White Man's society. This is hardly the case.

Josephine's mother had died an unfortunate death on the road, thus Josephine, an older brother and a younger sister were raised mostly by Grandmother, Caroline Supernault.

Luella and I remember Josephine as one of those good kids whom we learned to appreciate for her gentle ways. She tended to be timid about having to walk home after a visit that had extended beyond daylight. I remember her for her unusual

Fleuri L'Hirondelle

strength. Though she was of only a medium build she could bat a softball great distances with no apparent effort. In undue course she had a baby.

One Saturday she, some of her relatives, and I were in Peace River. That evening they returned to Little Buffalo, spent most of the night there and then continued on to their home at Matawasaw, the ghost-town which had been decimated by the flu of 1919.

Sunday, December 10 was an unusual day. Not only was it very warm and pleasant but I recall looking out the kitchen window early that afternoon to see flakes of snow falling, the likes of which I have never seen either before or since. They were great, about the size of a quarter, and extremely fluffy, settling to form a blanket of the fleeciest down. Their exquisite carpet was almost three feet deep.

At the Mission all was quiet and at peace during that whole day and evening. We were totally unaware that a dismal drama was under way right in our community.

That evening, having shut off the powerplant at the usual 10:30 hour, I was preparing for bed when the telephone rang. (We had about six or eight of the ancient box-type telephones that were hung on walls. These facilitated communication on the yard). Raymond Sparklingeyes was on the phone. "Would you take the bodies to Town?" Bodies? This was the first I had heard of bodies!

Upon learning a few details I went to Grandma Supernault's cabin. Others were there already, but where was Josephine? I was told she was still in a car parked near the door. Upon checking, I found her sitting in the back seat in an upright position. I believe the baby had been taken in already. I was not prepared to accept her death. Having brought her into the warm cabin, I laid her on a cot and proceeded with artificial respiration, instructing others to do likewise for her baby. At the same time, still others were to put tire chains on my Ambassador, and fill it with gas.

Having folded down the back of the passenger seat to make a cot, we laid Josephine on it and set off for Peace River. We left the baby for dead.

Raymond Sparklingeyes drove, accompanied by Harvey

Whitehead, the son of Josephine's Uncle Charlie. I continued with artificial respiration.

With snow lying deep, the trip was a true battle. Before we were ever to Cadotte the bands in the transmission were smoking. Somehow the car plowed through. (When we returned in daylight we could see a ridge of snow piled up on either side of the groove through which the car had passed. Snow had pushed to within a few inches of the hood ornament).

By 5^{am} we reached Three Creeks. From there we telephoned a doctor. By the time we left Three Creeks it was evident that there was little, if any hope. Josephine's body received air with greater difficulty and she exhaled with a noise not apparent earlier. But we had tried our best until then; we resolved to continue to try.

Dr. Marshall arrived at the hospital shortly after we did. She gave Josephine oxygen, but we were obviously too late. When Josephine died, I do not know. I am satisfied we did what we could.

Later, part of the story emerged. Early Sunday morning, unknown to the others sleeping in their cabin at Matawasa, Josephine, carrying her baby, had set off down the trail apparently planning to walk to Loon Lake, a hike of some thirty miles. Upon reaching some abandoned buildings at the "Hay Camp," about five miles from Matawasa, she had entered one walking, and left it running. In her haste, she had left her winter boots behind. Obviously this rational person had been startled into irrational behaviour, likely even at her Uncle Charlie's cabin already. After leaving the "Hay Camp" she had carried on toward Loon Lake, dropping baby clothes as she went.

When her cousin, Harvey, and her brother, Leonard, found her and the baby late Sunday afternoon, she was still able to speak (whether coherently or not I do not know) but was near her end.

Several things mystify me. Why would a strong young woman expire on a warm winter day? Why was the investigating Mountie so anxious to end his investigation at my house. He didn't even go to the scene. Why was it "necessary" that Josephine should die?

Josephine and her baby lie buried at Cadotte Lake. Many others do as well, but Josephine will always occupy a special place in our memories.

After our departure from Little Buffalo the frequency of funerals seemed to escalate. On several occasions I was invited back to officiate. Several are very fresh in my memory.

My good friend Fleuri L'Hirondelle was one of those to go. Fleuri had been the recognized, if unofficial, leader in the community. He was a trader, cattleman and the brains in most that went on. He followed in the footsteps of his father who in his turn had likewise served that area.

While working with animals one day, Fleuri succumbed, without warning, to a heart attack. When we had his funeral, many of the community paid their last respects. I was especially pleased that our MLA, Al Adair, made the effort to honour Fleuri. His presence underlined the esteem with which the man was held.

Fleuri lies beside his father on the land held dear by both of them. A simple memorial marker, assembled by his welder son, marks the place. It would give me the greatest of joys to see Fleuri again!

Certainly I didn't become involved in these situations and communities for any benefit to myself; but when one tries to help people there are usually rewards. Gestures of appreciation are rewards as are the friendships formed.

Fence posts being prepared for treating and planting for the Co-op fence

Chapter 16

Of Endings and Beginnings

In this chapter I wish to address the land issue, particularly as it relates to the Little Buffalo Farming Co-op. My treatment of this thorny subject will be brief and sketchy but the matter is inextricably intertwined with my story. A related matter that I would like to somewhat clarify is the involvement of the Metis, who tend to be overlooked.

At the time of our arrival in 1961 the population of our area was a fifty-fifty split between Treaty and non-Treaty people. These were the descendants of the original inhabitants of the region who had begun moving in from the Lesser Slave Lake region some 50 years earlier.

Josie and Antoine L'Hirondelle arrived from St. Albert in 1911 to establish a trading post at Matawasaw near what was then known as Prairie Lake. This lake came to be known as Lubicon Lake, likely from 'Laboucan.' Chief Laboucan was one of the original chiefs.

The L'Hirondelles were Metis, as were such later traders as Buffalo Bill, Andy Colson, Ed McGillivray, and Harry Lambert. A fact which should not be overlooked is the degree of goodwill and co-operation that existed between the Treaties and the Metis.

During those early years Josie petitioned the government on behalf of the first chief, Joseph Laboucan, for a reserve. As a consequence, government agents surveyed an area of 25 square miles for a proposed reserve. This reserve was to be half a mile east of the L'Hirondelle homestead.

In a letter dated March 7, 1961 to Honourable R. D. Jorgensen, Minister of Public Works, Edmonton, a request for a Metis Colony for the Lubicon area was also made. Apparently it was submitted by Josie L'Hirondelle on behalf of chief Joseph Laboucan and Daniel Calahesin (Metis). The facts that there was such co-operation and that there were normal entitlements of land conferred by squatters rights, seem to have been overlooked

Logs for the Co-op sawmill

by the World Council of Churches and other would-be intervenors.

The years passed but nothing ever came of either the reserve, or as in some instances in Alberta , a Metis Colony. During our early years, I was unaware of any tension between the groups, if indeed there was some. As far as I was concerned, they were all people whom I wanted to see helped onto their feet economically.

Circumstances in the community did not suggest a distinction should be made between the two groups. They were intermarried. Their manner of life was, in most cases, similar. The only real difference was what was in some government file in far-off Ottawa.

Several facts became evident early in our careers in our adopted home. For example: if you are going to take children from the former type of life and put them into schools, logic decrees they must have opportunities in their new world.

Another very apparent reality was that our new friends were no duds. These were intelligent, capable, and skilful people. If we were to be honest about the matter, we had to acknowledge that there was no way that the land could, in the traditional manner, sustain their rapidly increasing numbers. Was there something that could be done?

Meetings were organized to address such problems. We talked among ourselves. We brought in outside advisors and government officials. We considered all of our few options. We decided on cattle. Cattle seemed a viable proposition for several reasons. People, years ago, had run individual herds. The L'Hirondelles, even during our time, ran cattle. There seemed to be ample space and grass. There were people enough who were less than fully employed and could use jobs.

The greatest hurdle, of all things, turned out to be land. Our area had been designated "The Green Zone." It was part of the kingdom presided over by The Department of Lands and Forests. Their Number One Tenet was, "Thou shalt not farm in the Green Zone." There were those who determined that this was the way it was going to be. Well I remember M.D.'s promise, "You'll never get that land!" (Maybe it was Luella's good supper that made him feel so confident and pert).

In my books "never" is a long time. Fleuri L'Hirondelle was another who was less than impressed with this idea of "never." We had our planning meetings, and invited government advisors, forestry people, agricultural people, community development people, plus their cousins.

Harvesting an oats crop

Edward & Josephine Laboucan with son Michael

We met among ourselves at the local level. We sat many nights in that smoky classroom trying to formulate a workable plan. This plan had to be acceptable to the local people and had to be seen as workable by those who held the strings attached to both the purse and the land. These were the days of ARDA, a community development agency sponsored by the Alberta Government. Community development was not an entirely new concept.

During those years the people of Assumption marched in Edmonton. Should we be that militant? What might we do?

While I was heavily involved with the men in all of this, Luella was also busy. During the time this process was going on, the many people who came to our community had to be fed and otherwise accommodated. Because there was neither a motel nor a café in the community , looking after guests invariably became Luella's responsibility. We were best able to thus provide because our humble bungalow was the most spacious place in the community and Luella's cooking was always good. We've entertained them all from Hon. Fimright and Hon. Donavon

Ross, cabinet ministers, right on down the list. What fine people most of them were!

Nor did we stop at local meetings. In time, a delegation of us went to Edmonton. Those were the days of Harry Strom's Social Creditors. We presented our case, as best we could, before such people as Henry Rusty and Ray Speaker. Poor Henry Rusty. I didn't feel much sympathy at the time, but he must have become very weary of having his ear twisted through the whole lunch hour we shared!

Our begging paid dividends. By an Order in Council it was decreed that we get the freedom to use our land for agricultural purposes. We were also to be given a $178,000.00 grant in two stages! Eight years of effort were being rewarded!

I wonder if government money was ever spent more carefully than we spent ours. Each nickel was rolled over three times before it was given up.

The interminable meetings continued. Now the emphasis shifted from, "How do we get the help of Government?" to

One of the Co-op's first calves

"How do we run our affairs for the greatest benefit of all the participants?"

We called our organization "Little Buffalo Farming Co-op." A note of clarification should here be made. During my LaCrete years a group southeast of Peace River adopted the Little Buffalo name for their co-op which handled lumber. One winter they accepted delivery of most of a season's production of lumber by the Zacharias clan of LaCrete. Then they went broke, or something, and refused to pay. That was the end of the Zacharias mill. It should be noted that there was no relationship between the two Little Buffalo Co-ops. Our co-op did not pull stunts of that nature!

We, who worked in an advisory capacity, received no remuneration. Those who worked as labourers and equipment operators were to receive an hourly wage of three dollars. It was agreed that part of this $3 would be banked with the Co-op and later translated into individual assets, such as cattle, when sufficient collateral was collected.

One of the first things we did was go on a field trip during an Easter vacation when I had first taken my family to Meadow Lake. Most of the participants in this trip were the same men who had earlier travelled to Edmonton: George Ominayak and Edward Laboucan, both Treaties; Fleuri L'Hirondelle and Paul Cardinal, both Metis, and I (complete with the broken finger) the 'moniiyaw'. We toured several cattle operations, most particularly a feed-lot operation, near Bonnyville, where silage was being used.

Then we set about buying equipment and clearing land. One of the first machines we bought was a skidder which we hoped would clear willows and light brush as well as do field work. It proved too light so we hired Roy Alm with his crawler. We also acquired a John Deere tractor, tillage and seeding equipment, silage machines, a grader, sawmill and planer. We were in business.

Now any farmer will tell you that freshly broken land must lie fallow for a year before seeding. But we were on a roll, not to be deterred by convention. During that first late winter and spring we cleared land. (The brush was light and open places frequent).

Then we plowed and picked the roots, some by machine, but the men preferred to do it by hand. They built the fences; cutting, sharpening and treating their own posts. They seeded the newly broken land. Then we stood back and watched the oats grow. Grow it did! I have never seen anything like it. It grew as tall as a man! This crop we chopped into silage.

Then we bought cattle, a whole herd of cattle. We built fences, cleared land and prepared feed. The people were eager to work, provided they did not have to start too early in the morning. Sometimes we had more help than we could use.

It seemed we had a good thing going, but before long, problems began to emerge. They seemed to begin innocently enough. An Indian Affairs representative might appear in our community to offer a little financial assistance for this or that project. "Could you use a little money for windows? What about doors?" Certainly our co-op was in no position to be asking that kind of question. We were trying to become financially viable.

It was when I suggested to Fleuri L'Hirondelle that we continue our land development to the east of where we had developed and directly north of Lubicon Lake, that I became aware of his concern.

Fleuri was a wise man. He did not want to spend Co-op money on land that might slip out of our hands. He was obviously concerned the reserve issue was going to come to the fore.

His fears were well justified. The reserve question became a real issue in the community. A great rift developed. Co-operation was replaced with suspicion, and trust with fear.

The Little Buffalo Co-op farming project limped along for a few more years after the land issue heated up, due mostly to the efforts of Chester, Fleuri's son. He continued to work the land and different ones were hired to feed the cattle in winter. The good will and enthusiasm of earlier years faded quickly.

To me this is all a matter of great sadness and concern. The cattle are gone; the equipment is nonexistent or idle; the tremendously productive land lies fallow. Fleuri, that bastion of wisdom and stability, is gone. Yes, there is apparent progress. Our trail has become a fine broad highway. There are many new houses in the three newly established reserves. But in my mind, the concerns for the long term wellbeing of the people still persist. Questions come to mind.

Do modern politicians, bureaucrats, sociologists, liberal churchy types, lawyers and all other meddlers in the affairs of others, have any idea of where present policies and programs are taking us? Is it not unrealistic to expect that the multitudes of native youth will forever accept the sedation provided by paternalistic, seemingly generous philanthropy?

Is there not somewhere among us a statesman of principles, a leader who has a vision—who is motivated by ideals greater than myopic greed and short-term expediency? Where are the Sitting Bulls and Edward Laboucans of another time, who could offer insights and courageous leadership?

As for guilt-ridden white society, how can its judgement be respected? Most have no idea what a moccasin looks like; never mind having ever walked a mile in it.

Modern White sentiment, most often translated, "Government," is "If there is a problem, let's solve it by throwing a few more million dollars at it". Wouldn't it be nice if that were true? We could all continue in our soft roles and generate a little extra cash which the government could then relieve us of (as they do now except that the cash is not extra) and pass it on. Everyone would be ahead: the recipients would be laughing, the donors would have salved their consciences, and "government" would have bought a few more votes. Obviously this strategy has been anything but a help to the Indian people. Without the criminal bungling of the dominion government, many problems which exist in society in general and in the Native community in particular, would have been solved years ago. Unfortunately, the realities are somewhat more complex.

Even as I continue to work on this account in 1999, the land issue in the Little Buffalo area is not settled. The problem has been solved, in part, by the creation of three small reserves for the Woodland Cree at Simon Lake, Cadotte Lake and Marten Lake. However, those who chose to wait for a reserve, right at Little Buffalo, still wait.

Having made the foregoing observations and generalizations, let us again take up the ongoing thread of our story. As our twelfth year at Little Buffalo came to a close, we understood that the time had come for our family to move on. We had always planned to be the friends of all, but this was no longer possible with the political storms blowing as they were. The community was being torn into two factions. To be involved with one of the groups would soon be to be at odds with the other.

Another real factor in the matter of our move was the fact that Arlyn was going into Grade 9. We couldn't really handle Grade 9 along with the five other grades already being taught in one room.

Do we ever regret having spent those years hidden back in the bush? Not at all! Luella and I consider them to have been the most meaningful of our lives. People were helped; the children learned; we made many friends. When people continued to ask us to return, we knew we couldn't and were saddened by that realization. On the other hand, we are glad some still continue to indicate that warmth.

Today I go back to visit with decidedly mixed emotions. Are new houses, new roads and new schools necessarily evidence of the type of progress that gives hope? It is hope that enables the human. How can a human live without hope? And hope does not abide in what the person has at the moment. Hope is what the person sees when he raises his eyes to the future and beholds a vision that inspires him to present effort as he meets the challenges of his day. Yes, people can exist without hope, but can they really live?

Where my personal mental well-being is concerned, I prefer to remember the communities as they were. Have you ever noticed how, when people wish to remember someone, as in a newspaper, they prefer to use pictures taken during years of health and vibrancy?

Chapter 17

Some of the Near Misses!

Early in my flying career I determined that there was to be no "funny stuff." Observers may have wondered about the firmness of that resolution, but I usually considered myself a responsible member of the flying fraternity. Even though I endeavoured to conduct myself responsibly, there were times when matters could easily have turned out quite differently. Most of my closest calls occurred during my Little Buffalo years but there were incidents, as well, when I flew out of LaCrete.

A foremost problem I dealt with was navigation. The vastness of northern Alberta is impossible to imagine—and of course the bush does not end at Alberta's borders. A person might be trying for a fine strip out there somewhere using a most reliable plane, but if the pilot has lost his way, the pluses in the equation count for little.

This has all changed during these days of sophisticated radio equipment, and especially with the advent of Global Positioning Systems. These indicate exactly where a person is on earth and where he is going and even at precisely how many knots regardless of wind.

One early morning flight comes to mind. Weeks previously I had agreed to retrieve one of the trappers from Bison Lake on a certain morning. This was always a risky thing to do because there was no way of telling what the conditions would be, but I was committed and I like to make good on my commitments. The flight north was normal, but during the time I was picking up my man, a tremendous cloud bank moved in low from the west. During the early part of the return trip I could stay above it, but I had reason to wonder what was going to come of my landing if the cloud cover reached Little Buffalo before I did. Fortunately it did not.

Forest fire smoke and darkness were two other conditions which merited a lot of respect. Flying during the lengthening evenings of spring was fairly safe. Not only was one always getting more daylight than he had been used to, but darkness would come on gradually, if at all. The shortening days of autumn were another matter. Autumn evenings tended to catch me off guard.

Having to deal with doctors who had either not enough of their time or too much of mine was one problem. When I took patients to the hospital after school, I was expected to wait for the doctor's verdict. Then I had to check the patient into the hospital. The procedure took time.

Once, at least, the problem was aggravated by the bridge over the Peace River. This structure spanned the Peace between the airport on the west side of the river and the town on the east. In the good old pre-Big Brother days, all of us free spirits used to take our chances, and our turns on this long, narrow bridge. Passing was possible unless the other fellow happened to be a train. Then came the days of social responsibility when such freedom was no longer deemed expedient. Lights were installed on either end of the bridge.

One fall evening, I was in the normal snit to get home but—the light was red. I waited and waited, wondering how any vehicle could possibly take so long to cross one bridge even if it was across the Peace River. The answer, in time, emerged around a bend in the road in the form of a young lady on horseback. She had at her disposal all of her day and an unfortunate part of my night. I wonder if that was the night the people back home helped me by directing their vehicle lights down the strip as I landed.

The pilot flying into unattended strips can never be certain what surprises await him. One summer day when we no longer lived at Little Buffalo, I was going to visit some young summer workers there during a trip from Grouard to LaCrete. Fun was in short supply on that jaunt because wind gusts were very strong, especially near tree level. I would have been greatly relieved to get out of that jumping craft, but that was not to be my choice. Some local Kayooses were having a picnic lunch on our strip and were in no mood to desist. When I buzzed them, they jumped once and carried on with their grazing. After three or four such attempts to dislodge them, I had to accept the fact that they weren't going to be persuaded. There was nothing for it but to opt for the strip at Cadotte. It had neither grass nor horses.

The Bison Lake strip was certainly capable of surprises too! I had earlier agreed to deliver a trapper up there on a spring day which turned out to be particularly warm. As soon as I landed we realized that we had a problem. As I slowed to a stop the wheels sank four inches into mud. At least I was to have no load for the takeoff. If there had been a likelihood of frost I might have postponed my takeoff till morning, but frost was unlikely.

Whipping all my 85 Continental ponies into frenzied action, we roared down the strip. There was much roaring, but no flying. As always under such circumstances, the wheels picked up mud and threw it into the prop which in turn threw it back over the windscreen in particular and the plane in general. This was not a procedure designed to soothe nerves nor is it recommended in any flying manual I have discovered to date.

Taxiing back for a second try presented another problem because by then the plane was heating. However, with three local lads pushing on each strut we managed to get back to the end of the strip; actually we went beyond that. The soil on the strip itself had been disturbed and was for that reason very soft now that it was wet. The approach had been cleared of trees but the ground remained undisturbed. We took the plane back among the stumps and whatever in order to start the takeoff roll. Our chancy plan worked. By the time we reached the soft section, the plane was light enough that it did not sink.

By the time I was airborne, the windscreen was so plastered that I couldn't see a thing except through a tiny crack of about 1/2 inch at the bottom of the screen. So be it. I wasn't going to return for a window wash. Between my crack of visibility up front and a reasonably clean side window I reached home—again.

Ski flying is a joy well worth experiencing. One gains a sense of freedom difficult to duplicate. Lakes are everywhere; you need only take your pick but you had better be a bit choosy for there are a host of hazards that need to be taken into strict account!

For instance, I was once landing on Loon Lake when, although the day was fairly bright, an unusual visibility problem existed. It was impossible to discern where ice and snow gave way to sky. Fortunately I was near the shore. By looking out the side window and considering the location of the weeds, I could make the distinction.

Thin ice is also a potential problem. Luella flew only when she had a very good reason. One Sunday we felt that she had that reason. She had been housebound for weeks and a visit to Dunns in Loon Lake seemed a good idea. We landed on the lake and taxied up the river. Later, we discovered that only very recently had the ice begun to support traffic of any kind!

Ski flying into a confined area is another treacherous process, particularly if the surface is icy and there happens to be a crosswind. If the pilot does not create enough prop-wash, the wind catches the tailplane and causes the plane to head into the wind. That can be bad news if the wind happens to be blowing through a fence. When enough prop-wash is being produced to allow for rudder steering, thrust is also being produced. A little thrust and a lot of ice make a bad combination. Thus the pilot can take his pick. The right choice is not always apparent but he has to choose quickly. Time is not on his side. When a person has wheels and brakes, he controls the crosswind hazard by using his brakes in the steering process.

While the pilot is dealing with all these external factors, he does well to remember the plane has its own characteristics which must be respected. If a person has reason to assess an incident, when an accident does not materialize, one can never be certain which additional ingredients (and in what measure) would have brought it about. Stalls are one hazard to be avoided, particularly on takeoffs and landings. Speaking of close calls related to stalls, several incidents come to mind.

One morning I was taking Mildred Mallinger to Town. There was a little frost on the wings, but how could such a minor detail make a difference? I wasn't long in discovering! Mildred was no heavyweight—perhaps half of the weight of some people I have hauled, but that morning when we went to climb over the quickly advancing trees to the north, there just was not much lift in those wings. We had a perfect setting for a stall—low air speed, an obstacle, and not much lift. All one needed to do was get excited and pull back hard on the control column, a perfectly natural reaction when a bluff of trees is coming at you in a hurry. I lived to take frost more seriously. The hazard is usually attended to by working a rope to and fro over the wing surface.

During another trip, when I was hauling a load of trading goods into Bison Lake, the stall problem again raised its treacherous head. The weight of 25 pound lard pails tallies up quickly. I knew I was overloaded, but things had always worked out to that point in time, so I preferred to believe that I could get away with this situation too. Somehow I got off the ground at home, but once at Bison I wasn't sure whether I should land on the lake, near the cabins or on the airstrip about half a mile away. I flew low and slow over the lake checking for the normal hazards: hard drifts, overflow, cracks, etc. Banking too steeply in one turn, I suddenly felt the plane slip to the low wing. 50 feet of altitude doesn't allow for much recovery time. Fortunately several quick corrections overcame the danger, again!

One thing can certainly be said for those near misses; they are wonderful, even if somewhat curt, flying instructors.

Thankfully I was able to fly those hundreds of trips without ever scratching anyone except myself. I received one small bruise on my left leg. It came about in the following fashion.

Our community was obviously very isolated. We (Mildred Mallinger being then my co-teacher) thought it would be a fine thing to take our children to Edmonton on a field trip. We extended the necessary, "Please?" to the School Division. Yes, they would provide a bus. Then, the night before we were to leave, official wisdom had it that the road was unfit. It was news to us; the trail was frozen solid. This cancellation was a tremendous disappointment to our students and likely contributed to the illness of one of them.

In any case, he became ill on the day when we should have been on our way to Edmonton. I was asked to take him to the hospital. The hospital in Peace River must have been full, so instead of admitting the young fellow, the doctor prescribed a dose of penicillin and sent us on our way.

We had hardly left the airport when I realized we had a problem; the plane wanted to pull to the right. I slid over and looked out the right window trying to ascertain the reason for the drag. To my dismay, the cable and bungie, which hold up the tip of the ski during flight, were not holding. The ski hung in a tip-down attitude. I had no idea which way the ski was going to go upon making the inevitable landing. If it came up, there would be no problem: if it went down, it would dig into the snow, buckle under, and drive the leg into the snow. Since ambulances were easier to come by in Peace River than out at Little Buffalo, I decided to do what needed to be done at the Peace River Airport even though the conditions for landing were worse there than they would have been at home.

The situation at Peace River was not auspicious. Much snow had fallen. The snowfall, plus what had been blown off the runway, lay where I was going to land. Furthermore, the warmth of the February sun had softened the snow to a point where it would not carry the plane. Nevertheless, flying rule number one still held—what had gone up had to come down.

If I had been certain what that ski would do I would have been okay, but I did not know. If it was going to buckle under, I wanted to be going as slowly as possible. Thus I opted to come in at an awkward, left wing low, attitude, yawing to the right. I shouldn't have bothered. The dangling right ski came up but the left ski dug into the soft snow, buckling the left leg under, and tearing it from its bulkhead. There was further extensive damage to the left wing and propeller. Other damages were a bruise to my left leg and a rather large dent in my bank account.

The Ministry of Transport investigation discovered that a safety nut had been used too often and had come off, allowing the ski harness to fail. The fibre on such nuts deteriorates with use.

I should not fail to point out that there was a very crucial bright side to this story. When we realized that there was to be no more flying, we took the sick boy back to the hospital where he was then admitted. Under their supervision it was discovered he was allergic to the penicillin which had been prescribed. We wonder what would have happened if we had been successful in flying him home, and his family had continued to doctor with their medicine.

Regardless of the degree of caution exercised, the very nature of bush flying was hazardous. One of the major contributors to danger was a lack of proper communication. For instance, any pilot will tell you that the proper opening and closing of flight plans is a matter of utmost importance. Important, yes, but impossible too, when there are no telephones.

One Sunday night I was returning to LaCrete from Little Buffalo. As I went north the weather deteriorated, so I decided I would follow the pipeline which would take me to the Peace River which would guide me to Fort Vermilion (where there was a telephone). As I followed the pipe, the weather closed right in on me. I had passed an airstrip earlier, so turning as tight a 180 degree as possible, I headed back and decided to call it a day.

A little heated radio shack stood by the strip. I tried calling out from there. I had no idea about frequencies nor was there any way of telling whether the outfit even worked. At least I was warm. Pink insulation furnished some degree of comfort, or shall I say discomfort?

Usually, when a person figures he has made a great discovery he learns that someone else has already been there. This was again my experience; only this time the "somebodies" were "somethings." They had four scratchy little legs apiece, and they were not shy! Almost immediately after the lights went out, they were out of their holes in force. Unfortunately their chores often involved short-cuts across their co-tenant. Finally I left the lights on. The light inhibited their activities somewhat.

As was the case so often, Luella had no idea where her husband was or if, in fact, she still had one. This situation was particularly nerve wracking because she had made contact with Rose L'Hirondelle at Little Buffalo on Sunday night, discovering that I had left. (By the late 70's there were some telephones, even at Little Buffalo.)

In the morning at about eight o'clock, she contacted Jack Brock about looking for me. While still on the phone, Jack glanced out his LaCrete window and spotted me coming in. (I always hated having to spend time before school in that noisy staff room. I wanted to go straight to my classroom and get started!)

An interesting little aside to the foregoing account involves the white moose which stood on the pipeline just past the airstrip. I have often wondered if he was a true albino or if he had been stripped of his hair by lice. I'll have to check that one out with the angel who was on duty that day.

Very possibly the tightest squeak I ever experienced was right at home after a brief hop over from our Tompkins quarter section. So often it is those little hops that prove dangerous. If your trip is to be 200 miles you make some plans; if it is only 20, one tends to say, "Ah, well . . ."

Farmer's Day had dawned so there was to be no school. While the farmers had their day, I decided to have a day of farming over on the Tompkins quarter, about 20 miles away. Since everything I needed was over there already, I decided to fly over. Upon landing, I discovered a flat tire on a front wheel of the tractor. I took it off and, though it was plenty big, I put it beside my bucket seat in the plane. There was no good way of tying it down; anyway, it was just a short hop home.

There was no turbulence so the wheel rode well enough most of the way, but when the nose of the plane dropped on my final approach at home, that large, heavy wheel rolled forward. Now why I had the second control column in place, I do not recall. But there it was. By the time that tool of death had stopped its roll it was just touching the control column. The seat cushion well had caught it just in time. Had that wheel rolled even two inches further, someone else would likely be telling this story, because I was only about 50 feet up when this happened. Had the wheel thrown the plane into a dive, there would have been no time for recovery. As it was, with my right hand I grabbed the wheel and yanked it away from the controls while with the other hand I pulled up the plane in order to get reorganized for a second approach. Wow!

Part II

The Post Little Buffalo Years

Illustrative of early travel

Chapter 18

Development of Northern Alberta

I often say that without our tools we humans are a helpless lot. Even with the help of our gadgets we are still bound by time and space to relatively confined areas. If we have walked or driven an hour or, for that matter, flown an hour to get to work in the morning, we feel we have covered a fair distance. Maybe our own finiteness explains, in part, why it seems so inconceivable that the fellow standing beside the sign in Baker Lake, 200 kilometres south of the Arctic Circle is actually standing at the geographic centre of Canada.

Given the tremendous distances involved, transportation has always been a major consideration in the north whether movement was to be by water, land, or air, and regardless of whether we are talking about imports or exports. To complicate things, often the northern feature that would be a benefit in one respect proves to be a negative factor in another. The river systems are a case in point.

Had the river systems not been in place, northern development as we know it, would have been delayed by centuries. On the other hand, rivers are a very real barrier when they do not come complete with a bridge or, at least, a ferry. If we were ever inclined to doubt that fact, our doubts were thoroughly laid to rest early one frosty Monday morning.

On the preceding Friday night, Arlyn and Laurella had returned home from Prairie Bible Institute for Christmas. The temperature was about -50 degrees. They brought with them their Fijian friend, Kou Chiu.

Early Monday morning with the temperature at about –40°, we left for the dentist's office in Peace River. Never did it occur to me that at these temperatures there might be a problem on the ice crossing used by the children several nights previous.

But there was a problem, a serious one. Someone had tinkered with the Bennett Dam in B.C. causing overflow to gather on either edge of the Peace River. This overflow had frozen, but not to the strength where it would carry our car. In it went. Water covered the lower part of the motor and even the floor in front of the back seat. Obviously we were not getting out of the situation quickly, so our first concern was the temperature. Kou Chiu had no winter footwear to begin with and Arlyn was soaked to the knees after having tried to push.

No one had a match. Our best hope seemed to be a Department of Highways bunkhouse. I gained entry, hoping Highways people would understand. In the bunkhouse we discovered one lonely but very precious match, as well as a propane stove. Suspecting that the propane was not vaporizing at that temperature, we carefully laid a campfire outdoors and used our one hope on it. Fire! Wonderful warmth! By setting mattresses on edge around the fire, we were able to keep everyone reasonably warm. At least we were safe.

Having attended to that problem, we gave our attention to the car. After jacking the rear wheels up out of the water we laid planks under them, but any splat of water formed ice immediately. The car could not pull itself back up that incline.

Fortunately, others arrived on the scene after a couple of hours and pulled us up onto the bank. We were able to go, at least for a while, but our problems were not over yet.

A few miles later, the car quit. Assuming the gas line was frozen, I went to put alcohol into the tank. Upon opening the cap a sucking sound resulted. That was strange, but soon the car ran again—for a few miles. Then it quit again. Once more the sucking sound was apparent. Repeating this procedure at required intervals, we arrived home.

While we were in the drink, water had entered the breather line for the gas tank. When it froze, no air could get into the gas tank to replace the gas being burned. When a vacuum was created, the motor could suck no gas.

Our whole family was rather impressed with our little misadventure, but no one more so than Kou Chiu. Accompanied by a good deal of laughter, for Kou Chiu was a great story teller, he re-enacted the whole experience for the boys that evening in their bedroom. He was impressed particularly by his jeans; they had actually turned stiff. Never had he witnessed jeans acting like that in Fiji.

The development of Northern Alberta would not have stalled without the airplane, but development was certainly facilitated by its presence. To people living in isolated areas, air travel is a tremendous blessing in matters of convenience and safety. Industry makes good use of the plane too, as in the development of the Rainbow Lake oil field.

At one juncture during the 1960's, when I was making frequent trips to the Peace River Airport, I was greatly impressed to find there a mountain of supplies. Flow line, drill stem, barrels of fuel and other related piles of goods were stacked eight or ten feet deep. Someone had received a sudden urge to get the Rainbow Oil Field under way. Using two Hercules aircraft, they proceeded to supply the development. There must have been some compelling reason why they could not wait for frost and a winter road.

While one trip was under way, the ground crew would be preparing for the next one by loading a lowbed trailer. The loaded pallets were placed on series of rollers on the truck. When the plane returned, the lower part of the tail was dropped, the trailer backed to the open freight hold, and a winch cable extended from the front of the hold. The whole load was thus pulled in and the plane readied to fly. Load sizes varied between 16 and 22 tons. When extra thrust was required for takeoff, booster rockets were fired.

In short order, nothing remained of that mountain of goods but a memory. Rainbow Lake has since received its own paved highway which stretches west from High Level.

Another area in which aircraft are invaluable is in the area of forest protection. Even today, some fires are allowed to burn, but not usually in Alberta. Today aircraft greatly facilitate the early detection of fires as well as the fighting of them. Helicopters drop in firefighters to quell lesser blazes early. Planes quickly move crews about. Bombers douse the fires with retardant.

The result of better fire fighting abilities and procedures is that northern forests are in better shape than ever. The traveller may drive along many hundreds of miles of road observing the evergreens beginning to emerge from among the nurse crop of poplars. The poplars have enabled the coniferous forest to get under way.

Speaking of fire suppression, one Sunday as I approached Garden River, I noticed a forest fire in the Wood Buffalo Park. I assumed that there would not be many men at home that day. To my surprise they were at home. The explanation was that nature was being allowed to take its course. This seemed strange. I do not have the related facts, but it does seem strange that fine timber in the Park may not be harvested, for ecological reasons, or whatever, but fires are allowed to burn.

Where transportation is concerned we should not forget the lowly cutline. During the 1950's and 1960's thousands of miles of cutlines were cut for seismic crews as they sought oil. These narrow cuts, made by crawler tractors, provided woodsmen, particularly trappers, with travel routes. Their usefulness was underlined when some freak snowfall would bend the leafy deciduous trees across the cuts blocking passage. Considerable effort was required, on the part of a trapper who wanted to again open such lines, but had only a chain saw with which to work.

Since early travellers, particularly those of the fur trade, relied heavily on water routes, the land areas drained by the remotest streams of the drainage network tended to be reached later. This was the pattern of development in the area north of Lesser Slave Lake. The Little Buffalo region was settled later than the Lesser Slave Lake area, or indeed almost anywhere else in Alberta. This fact seems to explain why most of the Treaty people belonged to the Whitefish Lake Band. Whitefish Lake was nearer to a tributary of the Athabasca River.

Agricultural development followed the same type of pattern.

To this vast and diversified country came those in whose breast beat a heart of hope. Their backgrounds were varied and the expectations mixed but likely we can safely assume that they shared a common commodity—a spark of hope.

The absence of written history allows us to go back only so far. Living memory suggests that the first invaders were the warlike Cree of the south. Stories of battles in places like John D'Or Prairie and Fort Chipewyan are still retold. Tales of battles fought, and prisoners taken are well remembered. The Cree thrust extended north to the lower Peace River and west, just into British Columbia . Who knows what spurred them on? We can surmise that they were driven by the same objectives that drove the white people later—desire for land and its resources.

The next influx brought the fur traders. We know what spurred them on. Their coming altered the social scene, but the physical, hardly at all. A native can live in the bush for one hundred years and will leave hardly a mark. Likewise the fur traders.

They were followed by the Metis and White settlers. The earliest were drawn by the fur industry. Some were drawn by the land. Others were pushed from dried out southern farms. A few fled the WWI draft. Their origins were as varied as their groups. They came from remote Russia. Some came from southern Alberta. The rest came from places between. Many came; a few turned back. Those who remained were rewarded. We do not know what became of the disenchanted and defeated.

At first the settlers' marks were less obvious but the rate of change escalated. The little homesteads became prosperous farms; the little saw mills became huge mills. In the 1950's came the oil people. Soon the whole country outside the Cambrian Shield bore their imprint. Cutlines crisscrossed the landscape; pipelines snaked through the bush; trails became roads and isolated trapper's cabins gave way to growing towns.

Maybe most significantly, the flickering, faltering, sputtering, feeble hope barely alive in many a pioneer breast sprang to life. One success was built upon another. Gone are the days when Northerners cast furtive glances over their shoulders wondering whether retreat would not be advisable. We who work in the North have confidence; we have resources; we have abilities; we have a future.

Yet this drama needed time to unfold. Type setting for the emerging saga was a laborious process. In the following pages we will recount part of the story of one of the communities on the cutting edge.

Traditional Mennonite foods being prepared in outdoor ovens and traditional Mennonite "Mea Gropas" (food cookers).

Chapter 19

LaCrete During Its Early Days

The LaCrete area was an example of a region which long remained untouched. It was remote and isolated. Thus when the Old Colony Mennonites of such places as Manitoba, Saskatchewan, British Honduras, and Mexico heard of a remote yet arable area in northern Alberta, they thought they had found a place of escape. They were looking for a refuge far removed from secular society.

Education was a principal problem for these people. It was felt the children would be lost to their religious ways if they were trained in secular schools.

As the fur industry lost ground, the agricultural sector came to the fore. For decades there was a considerable overlapping, partly because neither enterprise was adequate to sustain the people, and partly because food production was important in maintaining the trappers.

Agricultural activity gained its first great impetus in the Fort Vermilion area with the coming of the Lawrences. (Others have dealt with this subject in proper detail). Their operation was upriver from Fort Vermilion, on the north side of the Peace. Buttertown, also a largely agricultural community, was across the River from the Fort.

There was less activity in the LaCrete area, it being several miles removed from the river. Settlement there was begun by a mixture of Indians, Metis, and Whites.

The memories of several early settlers are kept alive by such names as Savage Prairie and Wilson Prairie. The names of others are less readily remembered; the Wards, Cardinals, Tourangeaus. The core of LaCrete is situated on the homestead quarter of Louis Tourangeau who still lived there well into the 1970's.

Since there is often some confusion regarding the word "Mennonite," a word of explanation is justified. Often the term "Mennonite" is used as one would use "French"," English", or

"Jew." Jews are often thought of as a religious group, their religion being Judaism; that is, having to do with the Mosaic Law. They are, however, a people of a certain bloodline as are the French. The term "Mennonite" has very little to do with blood. In the true sense it has to do with faith. To be a true Mennonite is to be a born again, baptized member of the Mennonite Church which is an outgrowth of the original Reformation-Period Believer's Church. Menno Simons, whose name became part of the group's name, found the Lord through the witness of these "Anabaptists" and became the leader of the North-European Christians.

Today, even within Mennonite ranks, there is a great diversity of adherence to the basic evangelical tenets. The "Old Colony" element, which was dominant in the early settlement of LaCrete, is one sub-group. They are characterized by their desire to strictly adhere to their own particular code of behaviour in matters of dress, language, and form of worship. At one stage at least seven different varieties of Mennonites shared the name at LaCrete.

Whatever the religious persuasion, or ethnic background, if a person wanted to live at LaCrete he had to get there. That has always been a challenge. Even in 1998 there is still no land route from Bison Lake to LaCrete. The roads and trails north of Peace River Town simply disappear in the bush near Bison Lake. Road access to LaCrete must be gained either using the Mackenzie Highway west of the Peace River or by a relatively new highway linking Fort Vermilion and Slave Lake Town.

Travel into Fort Vermilion during the glory days of the fur trade and the Hudson's Bay Company was by river. The most sophisticated steamer to use the route was the D.A. Thomas. There was other traffic as well. One less official enterprise was referred to, with a touch of frontier humour, as the "Russian Navy." Some of the settlers assembled rafts at Peace River Crossing, as it was then called, and merely floated down river. Their accounts alone would fill books.

One detailed account of early settlement at LaCrete may be found in, *A Heritage of Homesteads, Hardships and Hope.* This book was written as a community effort under the auspices of the "LaCrete and Area Then and Now Society." It is, in the main, a compilation of family stories as they relate to LaCrete's story 1914–1989.

My overview will be of a cursory nature.

The earliest of Mennonite settlers settled at Carcajou, (the French word for Wolverine). Carcajou is a short distance upriver from the present ferry crossing at Tompkins Landing.
There they settled on flats, too near the Peace River. Spring flooding proved this area to be a poor choice. Pulling up stakes once more, people such as the Isbrand Friesens, Jacob Unruhs and David Fehrs moved inland about 50 miles and settled in the present LaCrete/Buffalo Head area.

The river continued to serve as the link to the outside. It continued to bring in settlers and a few goods. It provided an outlet for early farm goods. Animals and grain were for decades, the primary exports.

The beginnings of the LaCrete area settlement were primitive, but the ingredients of a prosperous community were coming together. The land was fertile, the climate favourable, the growing season adequate. Shortness of the season was offset by the length of summer days. Being so far north, summer nights, only twilight really, are very short. These pluses, taken together with a disciplined and skilful people, added up to success.

Furthermore, I often wonder if the Almighty does not have pleasure in blessing that community. Though the theology may not be 100% correct, there is an obvious desire on the part of many to do right. Not only is Sunday observed as a no-work day, but a number of other Christian holidays are also. Spring seeding may have just gotten under way, but when Pentecost or Ascension Days arrive, the community shuts down. Yet (or should one say because of this?) the crops are almost invariably good. Rarely does a swath lie out over winter.

Fortunately we were within walking distance of
home before we really needed the tractor

Chapter 20

The Ennses Arrive in LaCrete

In 1973, into this relatively well established community, moved Henry and Luella Enns with their four children. Having given the reader some understanding of where we were to live, let us return to Little Buffalo.

When it had become apparent our time at Little Buffalo was winding down, we listened with interest to the accounts of Bill Janzen who had spent some years at LaCrete as a teacher. In 1972, I flew to LaCrete and liked what I saw. Later I went back to buy a property. In the spring of 1973 we chose a site for our farmstead.

While we were moving into our new community, some wondered why we would move even farther north. Dad, in B.C., could never understand why we would choose to live 24 hours away. Luella's family likely wondered as well, since some 17 hours of driving in a southeasterly direction were required to reach them.

Two factors dominated our decision. For one thing, I wished to continue to contribute something to my Native friends. Also, we shared something of the educational philosophies and understandings of certain "do's and don'ts" of our neighbours-to-be. During a university Phys-Ed course, I had felt obliged to sit out a dancing session. I did not want my children to undergo such experiences. Joining the people at LaCrete, who shared some of our scruples seemed a partial answer to such problems.

It was not that there was no negative peer pressure at LaCrete; it was real enough there too. But the children were able to handle it. Either they found friends who stood by them in their manner of life or they stood alone. It was not always easy for them to live by the principles that our family planned to live by, but I can not say that we, as parents, ever had a reason to be disappointed in our children.

Having selected our building site in May, we hired an expert brick layer, not to mention an excellent wit, to build our basement. When our family arrived in July, things were in order so that we could commence framing, the brick basement having already been partly built. Mr. Nafziger was our head carpenter. He, several local young fellows, Arlyn, and I got to work. Arlyn was thirteen then, well able to drive nails. Lyndell, at five years, helped too. His contribution was a power plant. This was a rather crude device consisting of a plank, a wire spool, some electric wire, plus several other accessories.

The house that resulted became our home for 13 years plus a few summers. I like to believe that our children look back with pleasure to those years.

One of the positive features of our home was the large recreation room where the young people's group, to which Arlyn belonged, frequently gathered. At Christmas, we would have the teacher families over for a social in that room.

The favourite features of the play room were the ping pong table, fireplace, and pool table which experienced many games

We had spent the night getting back from LaCrete. It's Monday morning and time to prepare for school

of Polish pool, which our Polish teacher taught us. It was lots of fun, requiring not cues, but agility. Our home was close to town so it was no great matter for the children to come over to play. While we were building our house, we lived in a bunk house. The children slept in our tent trailer but as summer became fall, and fall, winter the tent trailer population tended to drop while the bunk house population mounted.

One evening most of our family went visiting, by way of acquiring a cat. While we were gone, Arlyn decided to explore the bush. While so doing he became disoriented. Fortunately he discovered some helpful neighbours on the far side of the bush. These people were kind enough to bring him home.

There was a rising of some eyebrows when we began to set up shop. "Such a big house? How will you ever use it? How do you know you'll like to live here, so far removed from everything? Gyproc? What's that?"

These were not matters of great concern. The house was adequate, but not fancy. By comparison with the houses being built there now, it is very ordinary. Certainly Gyproc has become a very common commodity.

As for living in a remote area, the wondering people would have certainly been set at ease had they had any conception of where we had spent the previous twelve years!

If we had not been so certain moving time had arrived I might have felt guilty about leaving Little Buffalo. As it was, the change was a relief. The dozens of burdens and responsibilities which had been a part of normal life had passed into the hands of others. Now I could go to bed expecting nothing more than a good sleep. I knew that there would be no call to become involved in the problems of others during the night!

While we were settling in on the farm, we and several other families were also settling in as a church community. During September of 1973 (we had arrived in July), the Elmer Hamms came to LaCrete to establish a church. Our family plus seven or eight other like-minded families, together with the Hamms, gathered in the school to begin what came to be known as the LaCrete Christian Fellowship.

In time, others joined us and it became evident that a meeting place was required. I was honoured to be the chairman of the building committee for part of the building program.

Building was an ongoing process. We would use a building for only a few years and it would be found too small. I was still stuffing insulation bats into the rafters when the invitation came to go to Meander River. Two times we added to the original structure. By now the main sanctuary seats about four hundred people.

Arlyn remembers it was in that church setting he learned some of his singing skills. Those skills paid his way through Bible School and Missionary Development Program. He spent his summers going on singing tours. He served his internship in that building and was there commissioned as the church's first missionary.

Lyndell was, in that building, also commissioned for service first to Tanzania and then to Papua New Guinea as a missionary with MAF.

This group also supported Lanna-Marie as she worked at His Mansion near Chicago, helping troubled youth. Lanna-Marie served as a counsellor.

Laurella, too, profited by her experiences in that church even if she never needed their material help in her activities.

As for our home, we regarded it as a 110 acre godsend. We were within two miles of our schools. The soil was fertile, but never sticky when wet. There was not a rock to be found. Some 40 acres of farmland gave us elbowroom. Off to the west and north was a fine spruce and poplar bush which formed an elegant backdrop to our farmstead. Beyond the bush lay our lake where we could canoe, windsurf, water-ski and enjoy nature. Allowing for a certain degree of bias, I still regard the setting as one of the prettiest in the community.

True, access to our farm was a bit of a problem for the first year. The approach to our home involved a drive down Lover's Lane. As the name suggests, this secluded romantic route with its luxuriant canopy of overhanging trees was better suited to purposes other than travel during spring run-off. During the first year or two we used our tractor when the trail was submerged, but then a road was built and the problem disappeared.

Part of my educational philosophy involved who was responsible for what in the classroom. Having done my fair share of sweating over books, it seemed expedient that others take their turn at learning. Thus, as long as my students were in the classroom, I expected both them and me to make good use of the time. But when they left at the end of the day, the spirit of the place would go too. I could never endure the boredom of endless checking of lessons.

Thus I rationalized that if I occupied myself with non-school activities when the students were not in class, I would be refreshed and ready for them when they were on the job. Thus boredom in the classroom was not a real problem for me. Often teachers long for Friday, or a convention, or an in-service or other such break. I rarely did. I much preferred to establish a routine, free of interruptions. That way we could all settle in and work. For that reason I regarded November as likely the most profitable month of the school year.

November involved no cold days, nor hardly any holidays; summer holidays and harvest were over. Christmas activities were only a remote threat. Hot weather and ball games were not a problem. We were not expected to spend a lot of time on tests. By then the classes and teacher had come to an understanding of how things were to be. Mostly we could just work and progress.

It was always a real joy to have the children progress. Progress in the junior high area, where I spent most of my time, was especially evident. The little grade sevens, who came to us, were a juvenile lot. Three terms later when they moved out of Grade 9, we could hardly recognize them as the same people!

Scholastically, the same held true; and nowhere did progress appear more evident than in Grade 9 algebra. When students arrived in September they hardly knew the difference between a -2 and a +2. Some would go on to achieve almost perfect scores for the year, even though they were given a heavy amount of material to master.

With only my classroom and my Sunday activities to be concerned about, I took great pleasure in my new-found freedom. I used this freedom to work. Work has always been a very real part of my life. In large measure, it is my reason for being.

The 110 acres on which we lived furnished ample opportunity for work. They also proved to be a base of operations further afield.

One first major project after the house was complete was the building of a stone fireplace and chimney. Armed with a ten pound hammer with a wedge shaped head, Arlyn and I set off for a gravel pit down by the river. There lay a great heap of boulders which had been screened out of the gravel as it was being crushed for the roads. I learned that most of those rocks could be split in two if the grain was recognized, and the pounding directed accordingly. The result was usually two flat surfaces that had a beauty each its own. Mr. Cornie Unger, the bricklayer who built our basement, was able to fashion a chimney from these rocks. With the remainder I built the fireplace (in my eyes one of the nicest), a wishing well, and a wall to front the veranda.

In winter the bush provided the boys and me with exercise as we prepared our firewood. The house had an oil, and later natural gas, furnace but we generated most of the required heat with wood.

Although the bush had been logged, enough trees remained or had regrown to justify further logging. After school or on Saturdays Arlyn and I would fire up the tractor, and to the delight of Wimpy, our Samoyed, spend time in the bush. Farm tractors are not designed as skidders, so progress was less than impressive, but with effort, a few trees could be skidded out per session. These trees provided lumber as well as skids. The latter were timbers 4" x 6" x 4' used by builders of pipelines to lay under the pipe as it was being welded together.

While the foregoing activities were going on, advances were being made in two other areas. The idea of summer Bible camps was catching on as was the idea that Christians have responsibilities in the matter of spreading the Gospel.

Riverside Bible Camp, which was situated off the highway between Manning and Peace River, had been in operation for years, but interest among the sponsors was beginning to wane. Furthermore, there were those who felt that the Bible end of things should be played down—a recipe for the certain demise of the place. As others stepped back, support from LaCrete came on strong. Friends of ours, the Cornie Thiessens, were often in charge. Numbers of times we were asked to participate in the camp program. I would be either the speaker or the camp director.

As time went on, the camping idea caught on at LaCrete. In time, LaCrete became a major force, not only in the running of Riverside but also in the operations of the Eagle's Nest camp near High Level. The participants involve not only the mother churches in LaCrete and their affiliates in High level and Tompkins Landing, but also such groups as the Canadian Sunday School Mission, people of Fort Vermilion and the Pentecostal Church of High Level.

A major emphasis of the Eagle's Nest camp is the provision of a camping opportunity for the Native children of the surrounding reserves.

Many of the ideas Evangelical Christians grew up with came as news to the LaCrete people as they came under the teachings of the Bible. These had not always been rendered in a manner intelligible to them. The matter of missions was one such concept, which over a period of time, has been heartily embraced.

Shortly after arriving at our new home I began reaching out to the Natives in their communities. On the one hand I hoped that other believers would help me, while on the other hand I desired that any such outreach would be seen, by the Natives, as a united effort. There was no point in creating more confusion than necessary.

Thus five church groups chose several delegates each, to form a committee. The principal contribution of this committee was to organize an annual missions conference in co-operation with The Northern Canada Evangelical Mission.

After some years these joint conferences were discontinued. The participating churches could justify running their own conferences. So, even though the joint conference no longer happens, the missions conferences continue to be an ongoing feature of church life in the LaCrete/High Level region.

Missionary outreach was a matter of interest and concern, but other areas of life were being brought along concurrently.

Work such as land clearing and construction using heavy equipment has long intrigued me. This interest was a major factor in my spending many dollars in land clearing.

All around me people were farming, so I got that urge too. Land clearing provided another fine opportunity for spending money. Through all LaCrete's years, beating back the bush has been a vital part of life in that area. As farmers need more land, and as sons come along and want farms of their own, homesteads are taken up, and the farming area expanded. I felt inclined to get involved.

Since I spent so much time, effort and money clearing land, while we lived at LaCrete, I will go into some details as to the procedures involved, including a note regarding the scarification process. The reader may find this information in Appendix A.

At one point we seeded 350 acres which we had opened up. Harvest was not a great problem. A large part of the canola never germinated until July when the rains came. By then it was too late even though the growth was substantial. Experiences like that taught me what most farmers know. Farming takes dedication, skill, time, and an interest. I lacked those attributes to varying degrees so by the time the boys left home, I was prepared to walk away from the whole operation.

The points to be raised on the plus side of our farming operation have little to do with profit, but there were some advantages in being involved. Farming gave me an opportunity to associate with many in the community with whom I would otherwise have had no dealings. One of the very unfortunate aspects of living on "Teacher Row" in an isolated community is that the teachers tend to be further isolated from the surrounding community. Lack of communication between the two communities is rarely, if ever, a positive situation. Though, in a sense, we were still "outsiders," we nonetheless made many friends in the larger community, friendships we continue to value.

The farm also gave me an abundance of reasons to be physically active. Often the "abundance" could have well been somewhat less abundant, but one of the challenges of life seems always to be the finding of a balance in such matters.

Most importantly, this involvement gave our children an opportunity to learn how to work. Life must be difficult for people who, in their childhood, never learned the disciplines and joys of work and must always force themselves to do what must be done as they prepare for retirement. I do not believe that the next holiday from work is a priority consideration in the lives of the Enns clan.

Indirectly, my involvement with land also contributed to the ultimate success of Vangard Realty Ltd. Vangard will receive some attention later.

Lanna-Marie (Chicago bound), Luella, Arlyn and Henry at the LaCrete house.

Chapter 21

Family Life at LaCrete

With the move to LaCrete came changes in the patterns of family life. School and sports affairs took much of the children's time. No longer did I play with them at recess. I merely took my turn at supervision along with the other 40 staff members. When we were at home, work occupied our time. We again enjoyed the freedom that comes with living near a wooded area on a farm. The lake which encroached on our property was an added blessing. We had an assortment of cats, horses, cattle and Wimpy. The story of Wimpy is representative of the animals, even though none of the others ever captured our hearts as did he.

After we moved to LaCrete, Wimpy joined us to replace our first Samoyed, Kona. He was a creature of singular intelligence and vibrant enthusiasm. For example, he seemed to sense, before I ever opened the door, when it was to be a day of working outside. By the time the tractor was rolling he would be in ecstasy! He must have watched the front wheels, because if they even began to roll toward the bush, off he dashed. The reaction was quite different if my route led off the property. He knew exactly where the boundaries were.

When we left him for a day or two, he lived up to his name upon our arrival home. He would be beside himself with unbridled joy, but not beyond whimpering a mild reproach. "Did you really have to stay that long? How was it that you left me?"

Usually Wimpy was on top of things, but one morning his courage simply evaporated. When coyotes came near the house they would sometimes play with Wimpy. He would oblige, but he seemed to know better than to let them lure him into the bush. But one morning some wolves put in an appearance; that was another matter. They remained on the road about an eighth of a mile from the house as they trotted in from the north, went to the south boundary of our property, did a turn and headed back north. Had they been coyotes, Wimpy would have had a variety of comments to make. In this case, he uttered not a peep.

I am certain he had never before seen a wolf. He carefully stowed his tail and made himself scarce at the back side of the house. When his end came near, he met it without complaint, but it was a sad day.

Normally, our activities took us in six different directions. We might make up to six trips to town in a day. Our idea of a family activity was to take a trip.

At home in LaCrete on the occasion of our 25th anniversary

Because of the unrealism and seduction of television, we postponed its introduction into our home as long as possible. Arlyn and Laurella hardly experienced TV in our home, but as the younger two grew, the pressure to own a set mounted.

At one point I made Lyndell and Lanna-Marie a deal. I would take them to Disneyland if they agreed to not having TV.

Laurella went off to the Inter-Varsity camp at Pioneer Ranch near Rocky Mountain House while the youngest two and I went to California. Arlyn must have been on a singing tour. Luella was at a writer's conference in Calgary.

We got off to an exciting start. Normally, if Luella was not around to help me navigate, Laurella could. (She always was the most informed member of the family in pragmatic matters). But I had left both of them in Calgary, so it was up to us Disneylanders to find our way about. Today Calgary is a greatly improved place in which to drive. Then it was a true challenge. Matters did not develop well that morning and we were too long getting out of Calgary. When we finally extricated ourselves, we had yet to drive all the way to the Edmonton International Airport to catch our plane. That old BelAir did some humming that morning, but we made it!

In California we had a good time. Lyndell was about eleven then, and that was the last time I could beat him in a foot race. We visited the San Diego Zoo and Knott's Berry Farm as well as Disneyland. We nearly went hungry when no one wanted our Canadian money. Finally I persuaded an unsuspecting young thing, who had not yet learned otherwise, that this was in fact money and we were able to eat.

One of the most memorable trips took us even further north. Some might have felt that we had experienced a fair portion of "north" already. We had—but there is a great deal of it to experience!

Usually when we went travelling it was to visit relatives in either Saskatchewan or at the B.C. coast. Because we chose to live in the north it seemed always expected that we do the driving. This time we chose to do our own thing as we drove the Alaska Highway to Dawson City, Yukon and Tok, Alaska.

We travelled with a camper on our Chevrolet truck. It was a

long trip, but I consider it one of the most interesting we have taken. Places like Italy have more to offer than one could ever absorb, but the northern frontier has a totally unique appeal. What can fire the imagination like the relics from the exciting gold rush era?

Much of Dawson City remains to this day—the wooden sidewalks, the theatres, some homes, and original buildings such as the banks. Some effort is made to re-enact the past for the tourists. We listened with great interest as an impersonator of Robert Service recited his famous poems, "Betsy's Boil" and "The Cremation of Sam McGee," at his cabin.

Further afield we witnessed continued extraction of gold with modern equipment and methods. One large abandoned dredge was of special interest. Yet interesting as such trips might be , they were but one aspect of life; most of our living had to happen at home.

As members of a young, emerging, dynamic, and impressionable community, our family had opportunities to make a difference. Older, more established communities are not readily influenced. To some extent, we were able to make the bed in which we were going to lie. The institutions, programs, activities, and affairs in general produced the environment in which our children were being molded. One of the matters of consequence was church attendance.

A battle many families face is the matter of church attendance. This has never been a problem with us. During our last years together as a family, I was more than likely off in some Aboriginal settlement making my rounds, but the others went to church and Sunday School as a matter of course. It was what was done. No discussions or decisions in the matter were required.

The children might easily have resented the disruption to normal family living that resulted from my spending so much time away from home during their childhood years. They seemed to accept the fact that I was not doing this for myself. Often before they went to church they would help me package literature in preparation for these trips.

Earlier I mentioned that doing this type of visitation was taxing on me. The schedule involved sacrifice for my family too. It meant family-type Sunday activities were often ruled out. The children were "fatherless" and Luella attended church alone with her sometimes restless children.

An account of one incident will help to draw into focus how things were. I'll ask Luella to tell the story.

Lyndell became so ill that he lay in bed with a fever, and stopped eating. He was very thirsty, and Lanna-Marie kept taking water to him. His eyes were sensitive to light, and he broke out into a rash, so I thought perhaps he had measles. The public health nurse thought the rash looked like something different, and advised us to take Lyndell to a doctor.

We took him to a doctor in Fort Vermilion who immediately admitted him to the hospital and started intravenous because he was very dehydrated. The doctor didn't know what the problem was and we didn't realize how seriously ill Lyndell was.

Sunday morning, Henry and Arlyn flew to Little Buffalo to do some visitation. The girls and I went to church in LaCrete. I was called out of the service to see the Public Health Nurse, who informed me that the doctor had called to say that he wanted to send Lyndell to Edmonton, and if I wanted to go with him the plane would wait for me. Menno and Elvina Hamm took me to Fort Vermilion and took the girls home with them.

The doctor was afraid that Lyndell might have meningitis, so he wanted to send him out as quickly as possible. Lyndell was on a stretcher and a nurse and I sat nearby in the small plane. It was a very windy afternoon, causing the roughest flight I have ever had, and making Lyndell sick to the stomach.

An ambulance took us to the Charles Camsell Hospital, where the doctors proceeded to do a spinal tap to test for meningitis. That was one of the hardest things I ever had to do; to sit and watch my child being tortured. Fortunately he did not have meningitis, but the doctors didn't know what he did have. During the next few days various specialists examined him. They would poke him and ask, "Does it hurt here?" until finally he said, "It hurts every place!" He was still on intravenous, and had three kinds of rash at once, so they took photographs to study the different types. One afternoon the fever must have peeked causing hallucinations. He appeared to be sleeping, but at intervals he opened his eyes as if to check if I was still there, and he told me what he saw. Once it was a man on the outside of the wall, once fire in the sky, and the third time he said, "I saw you in a garden. You had a white dress, and you looked nice." Then I was really worried: I thought he was dying and was seeing angels in heaven!

After that he slowly improved. Finally our blood test results arrived, and showed he had the same flu I had earlier. The doctor concluded that Lyndell had an allergic reaction to the flu. I went home after spending a week in the city, but Lyndell had to stay another week because his eyes were very sore. Then they put him on a plane to Peace River where we met him. I can still see that small eight year old boy, wearing dark sunglasses, walking from the plane to the terminal building.

I find this account of Luella's sobering for it points out again how easily life could have been very different. I do not believe we can assume that someone else would necessarily be doing Lyndell's work, influencing people for the Gospel a world away, had Lyndell not been given his opportunity.

Going back to the idea of our family life being disrupted by my frequent absences and the children choosing to understand and be co-operative, I believe Alfred George's observation is instructive.

Alfred George Chalifoux was one of my Grade 4 students at Meander River. By the time those little people had retrained their teacher, I had mellowed. I spent lots of time telling them stories and visiting. Through this sort of thing the children learned about life beyond their reserve and we also firmed up our friendships.

One account involved a mention of the fact that my youngest two children lived in Chicago, "Bull's" country and Tennessee. Alfred George asked if I wasn't worried that they might get into trouble such as using drugs. I don't suppose such a thought had ever entered my mind.

Luella and I are ever so thankful to our children for not causing us headaches with misbehaviour. Things could have been different!

Surely one of the greatest curses to be visited upon mankind is television. Few influences have done as much to normalize immorality as has the tube. It's successor, pornography on the Internet, will likely have an even greater negative impact on morals. As for virtual reality, it scares me.

True, "There is no new thing under the sun," but in former years a Robert Latimer* could have done as he did in some corner and maybe only his immediate community would know. With the help of the media a Latimer's behaviour is not only publicized throughout the world, but he is also accorded a certain celebrity status by moral revisionists who wish to promote their platform. A classic example of this reality happened during the current Olympics.

Ross Rebagliati had won a gold medal in snowboarding which sport had been introduced to the games for the first time. He was, however, temporarily relieved of his trophy when it was discovered that he had fooled with marijuana. When Canada yelled loud and long, the demoted hero was given back his medal. The immediate and joyous reaction from a representative of the "pot" community was unbridled enthusiasm. "He is rich; he is good looking; he is famous!" in other words, "What a representative for our cause!"

On his return trip from Japan, he was given favourable exposure during a personal TV interview conducted in California. Endorsements keep rolling in as his honours increase. During a recent Juno awards ceremony he was given special recognition.

Nevertheless, whatever one's opinion of the tube might be, it is a fact of modern life. In time, we all agreed times had changed and that a TV would be acceptable in our home. If we had to choose between a tube and resentful children we were prepared to accept the former.

An additional observation should be made with reference to TV. If there is going to be one in the house, and surely one should be adequate, it should be where it can be easily monitored. How can children be expected, on their own, to make

**Robert Latimer gained a degree of notoriety or fame (depending on one's position on euthanasia) for asphyxiating his 12 year old handicapped daughter.*

proper use of the off switch—especially in the privacy of a bedroom or basement?

Actually, there was not a lot of time for TV; there were other activities to occupy the children. School sports activities were an important aspect of life during those years. Admittedly, I did not contribute as much in that area as I might have. I always pled busyness. I could have been more supportive, especially where Arlyn was concerned. I always assumed my support in whatever the children chose to do was a given. I had not yet understood how important it is for children to have their parents present when they participate in sports. I had, however, understood that it is a good idea for fathers to take their sons fishing.

Only about an hour flight north of LaCrete, up on the Caribou Mountains, lies Margaret Lake with a fishing lodge, boats, and an airstrip. Arlyn and I spent parts of two days up there. We never caught any fish, but that was not the purpose of the excursion anyway. Furthermore, I never enjoyed cleaning fish. In any event we can record for posterity the fact that we went fishing.

Time was passing; the children were maturing. One by one they approached the scattering stage. Arlyn was the first to go. We realized that his going was to be only the beginning. In recognition of this fact, we wanted to do something special as a family. That was the occasion for the Yukon trip which has been mentioned.

After Grade 12 he went to B.C. where he worked in a lumber camp for a few weeks. When September came, he left that job to move to Bible school at Three Hills, Alberta. He spent the next five years there, four as a student and one on staff as a member of the King's Messengers Quartette. Their group toured in a public relations capacity for the school.

This time was followed by his training session on Vancouver Island in preparation for his missionary career.

When the children of Little Buffalo commiserated with Arlyn for not having parents, just teachers, they might have extended further sympathy because of his also being the son of a workaholic father. Life wasn't easy for him as he was expected to work hard, often in the cold. Why all this work was so important to me, I'm not certain. I like to feel that some of what Arlyn endured toughened him for the extreme tests he has endured as a missionary in Fort Chipewyan. Life isn't easy yet, but now he has his fine wife, and our first daughter-in-law Ann (nee Walton, of Oregon) to share his life.

Also, we are thankful that through the generosity of his home church in LaCrete, Arlyn and Ann have a decent home to live in. (Now, at least when they are home, they don't have to try to cook in those soggy willows in the flood flats at the end of Lake Athabasca.)

When houses in the nearly abandoned mining town of Uranium City became available I made numerous trips there trying to establish myself in the resale of those many fine homes. If I was flying alone, I would likely stop to visit Arlyn who was on my route. At one point he ran out of propane before the winter road was in and was trying to do his cooking under some soggy willows. What a pathetic scene!

He has been out for several furloughs during which he obtained a Masters in theology from the Baptist seminary in Edmonton.

Laurella, the one of the big smile and the cheery, even, disposition, was the next to go. Her itinerary also included Bible school at Prairie. During the summers the Department Of Highways had the good fortune of her help in road construction.

Another segment of her maturation process involved a stint in Europe. By way of familiarizing herself with that part of the world, she took a position doing maid-type work in an Austrian castle which served as a hostel. Next she took her nurse's training at Red Deer College.

During those years, while they were at a youth conference in Washington, she caught the eye of one Brett Joyce. In order to stake his claim, Brett rode his motor bike from Vancouver to LaCrete when he came to visit. One could say he paid his dues as he learned a major geography lesson. Some of his wooing was by telephone. We still smile as we remember the time deaf old Dad answered the telephone and thought it was Luella who was being asked for, so he called Luella to the phone.

"Hello, good looking!" was the cheery greeting. Mom likely felt flattered, but a bit chagrined in Brett's place when she realized that Dad should have understood "Laurella."

Having surmounted a few minor hurdles, Brett in time, became a husband, a father, and a member of the Enns family. Brynn and Kieran were later added to our number. I was going to describe them as little boys but they insist on becoming "less little." Both have already amassed amazing amounts of knowledge. Kieran is in kindergarten and has taught himself to read. Both lads pursue books with fervour. I hope they will go to schools where excelling is not considered a vice. If they don't, school is going to be a tedious experience.

At the time of this writing, Laurella is taking refresher courses in preparation for a return to nursing.

By the time Lyndell came along I had begun to understand it is important for children to have parents attend their activities. On several occasions I took him to his sports competitions.

He and I flew to Grande Prairie once, so he could compete in the Zones cross-country run. That was the time when some person, (I can't call him a spectator for he surely had his eyes clamped shut) stepped into Lyndell's way as he raced and caused him to fall. Fortunately, sports was a passing phase of his life. There were more pressing and worthwhile projects to occupy his talents.

Prairie at Three Hills counts among its schools a fine high school. We wanted our youngest two to take advantage of the superior training offered there. Lyndell went there for grades 11–12, while Lanna-Marie took her whole high school there. During those years at Prairie, Lyndell decided to go into mission aviation. Moody Bible Institute in Chicago offered the best program, so that is where he went after his high school graduation. Competition for places in the program was stiff. He felt he would have a better chance of being accepted if he took his required two years of Bible training at Moody.

The thirteen hour drive between Three Hills and LaCrete was always a fair sized chore, but travel between LaCrete and Chicago was yet another story. Customs was always a problem. We could ship no parcels across the line unless there was someone at the border to receive the goods. When he left for Chicago the first time, Lyndell had to try to take all his gear with him on the plane. Fortunately, on his first trip a helpful guard at the airport helped him with his baggage and also helped him find his way to within a few blocks of Moody. Even then he was not quite home-free because some local dudes let it be known that he was hiring them to help him out with his boxes whether he liked it or not.

Before he had to go back for his second term, it was agreed that a motorbike would ease the transportation problem. Accordingly, Brett was commissioned to locate one. He found a proper beauty in Vancouver. The tale of that Honda Interstate has a rather dramatic beginning and sad conclusion.

Lyndell was busy with his summer highways job, so Brett located the bike. Luella and I went there with the pick-up to get it. After we had it loaded, I crossed into Washington State to do a little shopping and sightseeing. No one seemed concerned when I crossed the border so I relaxed and proceeded to take a little tour which unfortunately took me toward the wilds of Mount Baker. Suddenly a light started flashing behind me. When the patrol officer came up beside me he was obviously concerned. As he checked my papers, he squeezed up tightly to my truck, lest he get shot, I suppose. (One can not be too careful with those wild hombres from Canada.) Having done his check, he invited me to follow him back to customs. I began to understand these lads were not playing games. Assuming my most subservient demeanour (I'm not good at that), I trotted out my best story about a son in Alberta who had not yet registered his new acquisition and a son-in-law in Vancouver and a wife in Abbotsford and a destination in Saskatchewan and . . . finally the customs people phoned Luella to get the same convoluted account. Since the details matched they decided to let me go on condition that I not return for five years. Signing such an agreement seemed a very acceptable alternative to waiting in a "clink" for a Monday court appearance.

Having taken his two years of Bible in Chicago, Lyndell then went on to Tennessee where he took his airframe, power plant, flying, and avionics training.

The Honda's demise transpired in Tennessee. Lyndell and a passenger were on a winding country road when they overtook a farm wagon and tractor. Just as Lyndell pulled over to pass this farm outfit, a patrol car turned into his lane. The resulting collision totalled both the car and bike. Lyndell's passenger was fortunate in that she received only scratches. Lyndell sustained a cut which encircled an eye. Today not even a scar is apparent. His guardian angel was distinguished by his alertness.

We replaced the bike with one bought in the U.S. and again there were border crossing problems. Lanna-Marie was with Lyndell when they tried to cross into Canada. The only way they could get into Canada was to promise not to use the bike in Canada other than to return to the U.S. in fall. What a tribulation! Lyndell needed wheels in the worst way to travel to his highways job but the bike had to sit.

His adventures in Tennessee, Tanzania, Australia, and Papua New Guinea would fill another book. He will have to write his own.

It was in Tanzania that Lyndell met Daniela—a dear Italian lass who is now our daughter and mother of two of our grandchildren, Lorenzo and Lezley.

Today you can communicate with their cause at www.powertochange.com. Lyndell and Daniela are with Momentum, an arm of Campus Crusade. The objective of Momentum is to reach people with the Gospel through the Internet Ministry.

Lanna-Marie, our little brunette, was the last to join our family. She never pushed forward, so by the time she had her turn there often wasn't much time for her contribution. Maybe that's how she came to be a master of the "comprehensive comment."

When she and her friends got together to play games she might be noisy enough, but her tendency to quiet observation sometimes caused her to be overlooked until she produced some achievement like leading her class in high school in both driver training and typing.

She used to take our car on the 700 mile trip to Three Hills when she was in high school. During one of her last trips home she stopped at the Red Rooster in Peace River for gas. When she went to pay for the gas, the lady wondered if she was sure she was old enough to drive. She had been doing that trip for years by then. We saw no problem. Her mother did have a problem, however, when it came time for the youngest one to go to Chicago.

Because Lanna-Marie was the last child to go, her final departure for Chicago was likely the most traumatic. We were already somewhat wiser. We had no plans to allow Chicago lads to offer her their "services" as had happened to Lyndell. Accordingly, it was decided that Lyndell should see to her transportation. Lyndell's second Honda, one of the 1100cc persuasion, was for its part certainly up to the task, but it is a long haul between LaCrete and Chicago!

Morning had come early that day when Lanna-Marie was to set off into an even wider world. In preparation for this trip we had built a trailer for the bike. Lanna-Marie's suggestion that it looked like a coffin did not reassure Luella. Lanna-Marie, true to form, was wearing shorts when they set off. At least they would telephone every night as they progressed on their way to Chicago. Luella remembers that morning as one of the lowest points of her life.

Today Lanna-Marie makes her home in Chicago where she continues to work in Moody's Correspondence School Department as an instructor.

Chapter 22
LaCrete Today

The Enns family was only one of many busy LaCrete families. By the time of our arrival in 1973, the community was well established. True, there was still no water and sewer in town; Carl Friesen's farm which is now in the middle of town was then out in the country. But the roads had been gravelled, and people only rarely got stuck in the middle of the highway. We were a community on the move!

Before moving on to a history of recent developments in the LaCrete area, a consideration of the name seems warranted. Considering the inhabitants of the region one might have expected a name like "Schoenthal" (Pleasant Vale), "Tiefengrund" (deep soil), or "Reinland" (clean land). (Indeed Reinland was the name used by the Low German settlers until overruled by the Post Office Department.) Any of these potential names would have reflected the deep respect of an agrarian people for the soil.

The French name has its genesis in World War I. Canada was aligned with Britain during this conflict but because feelings were not that cordial between the French and English, three Rivard brothers from Quebec wanted no part of the conflict. They fled the draft by crossing overland from Quebec to Peace River.

The largest of LaCrete's several sawmills

Having gained the river they used it to travel to a point five and a half miles southwest of LaCrete. There on the banks of the river they hid. An uncle in Fort Vermilion sometimes brought them food.

On the bank of the creek near which they lived was a hogback which reminded them of a rooster's comb. A rooster's comb in French is "la crete," hence "LaCrete." The degeneration of the original into the later "La Crate" would be due to a local habit of being somewhat less than precise in the pronunciation of vowels. The remaining French influence is mainly confined to bilingual signs at the post office.

A consideration of the family names in the book, *Homesteads, Hardships and Hope,* reveals an interesting pattern. Early references include Fred Tourangeau, the Rivards, Al Gradngenet, John Gibb, Alphonse Cardinal; the Lawrences, Halletts, Wilsons, and Sandersons. As the book progresses this assortment of names gives way to names which are traditionally "Mennonite". One has to wonder why such an unusual phenomenon transpired.

Obviously a major transition had taken place prior to our arrival in 1972. The already mentioned book does that subject justice. This writer will merely mention that it occurred.

When our family first visited LaCrete no café existed. To Mrs. Knelsen it was apparent that these wayfarers had been enroute for some time. (Actually anyone who arrives in LaCrete has been enroute for some time.) She graciously served us "faspa," the traditional Sunday afternoon lunch which includes many Mennonite dishes. This gesture was timely and appreciated, especially when, as things worked out, we had to spend all night on the muddy trail trying to get home.

On our way back to Little Buffalo we were to have a night's worth of mud problems. By about seven o'clock in the morning we were within a few miles of home, so I walked the rest of the way and got the tractor. With it we were able to get the pick-up and its occupants home. At least we were not too late for school.

The matter of cafés has changed. After several years the Penners renovated the White Farm Equipment building and started their business. At the time I wondered who at LaCrete would ever patronize a restaurant. Outsiders rarely came to Town and local people ate at home. I need not have wondered. In time Kay's would fill with loyal customers.

Other eateries followed—Lloyd's, Wiebes', Peters'—and they all did well, it seems.

As various businesses began in those early years, I must have lacked faith as I thought, "Who at LaCrete will ever support this or that business?" This question came to me when Knelsens brought in their first readi-mix truck. "Which thrifty LaCreter is going to pay for pre-mixed concrete?" Again I needn't have wondered. Soon there were two more pre-used mix trucks. Within a few years they were replaced by new units, and their numbers keep growing. In fact, this business thrives not only in LaCrete but in High Level as well. Modern LaCrete businesses are further highlighted in Appendix D.

While the business sector has moved forward aggressively and skilfully, the areas dependent on government dollars have tended to lag. LaCreters are more skilled at exercising individual initiative than begging. Furthermore, they tend to vote "incorrectly." Even so, much effort has been made to meet the medical, educational, social, recreational and spiritual needs of the community. The sorest spot, where public funding is concerned, has always been the matter of a hospital.

Meeting the medical needs of such a remote and scattered populace has always been a problem. The modern situation is a vast improvement over the state of affairs which prevailed during the days when Dr. Mary Jackson tried to serve from 70 miles and one wide river away. Yet by modern standards, much could still be desired. People like Alma Janzen have battled for years trying to get the government to build a hospital in LaCrete, but the nurses' clinic is about as close as they got to success. In other words, if you happen to live in Tompkins, some 50 miles south west of LaCrete, you had better not plan on getting sick or having an accident, especially during the time when the river is either freezing or breaking up. A trip to High Level, if required, is about 100 miles. Some stop at the hospital in Fort Vermilion which is closer.

Recently several dentists have begun practising in LaCrete.

An area which the local people address with both enthusiasm and pride is the care of the elderly. Quite independent of government assistance they have built and maintained a care facility where their aged and infirm are accommodated.

Most educational needs are attended to by the Fort Vermilion School Division. LaCrete itself has a high school plus two other schools for the junior grades. Other schools for the larger business area are located at Blumenort, Blue Hills and Buffalo Head Prairie. Three or four private schools function within the region.

Church attendance is a practice that is still cultivated rather religiously. The original dominance of the Old Colony persuasion has been heavily affected by the arrival of Mennonites and others who have somewhat different understandings. Closely akin to the Old Colony position are the Sommerfelder adherents. These two groups worship in about six buildings scattered throughout the community. Two large evangelical congregations, the LaCrete Christian Fellowship and the Bergthaler Church, worship in town. The Bergthalers also have two congregations which worship in nearby country communities.

In the Old Colony tradition, sports were viewed with suspicion and generally left out of the scheme of things. In more recent decades, as the youth have come along with views somewhat modified by a more modern scene, change has been demanded. These changes and facilities have been financed to a major degree by some government monies which somehow managed to filter through—a phenomenon of recent vintage. Thus LaCrete now includes in its recreational roster: parks, a tennis court, bowling alley, ice arena, curling rink and golf course. The schools have the expected recreational activities.

Yes, the hamlet now has water and sewer! A well was dug at the Peace River and the water is piped the eight miles to town where it is treated at the plant and distributed.

It is my pleasure to be a contributing member to the community. When I see former students successfully engaged in this or that venture, I like to think their Junior High experiences were a positive factor. When I see block after block filling with homes and compare that performance with what is happening in many other small towns I feel happy and rewarded.

Chapter 23

Continued Involvement in Native Communities

As I scan my life in retrospect an interesting pattern of 12's emerges. 12 years were required to complete Grade 12. Between 1950 and 1962 I was in preparation for my northern experience. 12 years at Little Buffalo were followed by another 12 at LaCrete Public. Although the divisions are not precise the suggestion is there.

Even though we moved from a predominantly Native community at Little Buffalo to the predominantly white community of LaCrete we had no intentions of forgetting our original purpose of trying to contribute to the Native Community.

Soon after our move, we came to understand that we were now surrounded by about a dozen Native communities of four different tribes. To be sure they were at a distance, but within reach. I wished to somehow establish contact with these people. There was no problem with Little Buffalo and Cadotte Lake; I was well known there. The other communities were strange to me, and, of course, I to them.

The distances involved and the briefness of time available dictated that most of my travel be by air and mini-bike.

The bike had small wheels, an air-cooled motor and collapsible handle bars. It would not fit behind the regular airplane seats so I removed them and replaced them with a single seat for myself. During earlier years my pilot's seat consisted of a wooden chair—less legs—plus a few cushions. In later days, aircraft maintenance people bolted down a proper bucket seat. The mini-bike could thus ride beside me.

During my visits in these Native communities, I distributed such periodicals as Muskeg Moccasingraph and Indian Life magazines plus Sunday School papers. Audio tapes were also very popular. In more recent years there were videos. One circuit might involve knocking on 350 doors.

Generally I visited one village on a Sunday, except in the case of the Tall Crees when both communities could be covered during one trip.

After only one or two visits, I realized the little strip at South Tall Cree was inadequate, so that destination became a road trip. (Even today, I smile at the remembrance of the time I gave an audio tape to one of the old gentlemen at South Tall Cree. I told him that it was in Cree. After taking it and solemnly contemplating it for some moments his comment was, "White man does everything.")

I was well aware that this visitation would not bring about any great, sweeping changes—but maybe I could bring a little light, a ray of hope, an insight. Maybe if I went ahead someone else would follow.

During 1983 and 1984, Arlyn again lived with us and was able to spend time visiting the three communities of John D'Or, Garden River and Fox Lake. He would have liked to reside in one of those communities but when he understood living in these communities was not allowed, he was placed in Fort Chipewyan. His occasional Cree video distributions and such to Garden River and Fox Lake today are usually made from the northeast by boat.

After Ann Walton, formerly of Prairie Bible College Faculty, married Arlyn in 1993 she joined him in Fort Chipewyan from where they continue their evangelism and teaching ministries.

Surely this self-assigned task of visitation was one of the toughest jobs I ever undertook. Was it the cross-cultural aspect of these visitations? I don't know. What I do know is that it was exhausting. It usually took until Wednesday to become somewhat rested.

One session in particular comes to mind. The airstrip at Fox Lake was built at right angles to the Peace River. I parked at the east end of the 1 1/2 mile runway. The community itself was scattered in several directions; the trails met where the public buildings were grouped. One day, as I followed a trail which followed the River, the chain came off my bike. Having no wrenches with me, I was reduced to pushing. The machine was not designed for pushing; the wheels were too small and the handlebars too tall. The thought came to me, "I wonder what God thinks of this effort?" I still wonder. Though I can wait to find out, it will be with interest that I listen to the Lord's appraisal of that and similar efforts. Any commendation will be appreciated.

Arlyn feels the preliminary canvassing I did in these communities makes his continuing evangelistic efforts easier. He is more apt to be regarded as a helpful friend.

Usually I was politely received, and in some of the homes there would be a cup of tea or even a meal. A few of the old people must have thought me something special. Certainly I never thought of myself as one to be revered.

Looking back on the thousands of miles of travel, I am thankful for safety. I do not remember ever turning back due to weather. Things might have been different. An incident involving the tail wheel on the plane might be illustrative.

At LaCrete I parked the plane by the house. Getting to the strip involved taxiing down our lane and then down the little-travelled country road to the airstrip. Having done all that one Sunday, I flew to Fox Lake where my landing was normal. I had taxied almost to where I was planning to park when suddenly the tail dropped. The whole tail wheel assembly had broken away from the fuselage. Was this a consequence of metal fatigue, or had I hit the sidewalk at home as the tail swung around? Anyway, I was down to two wheels.

Salvaging the spare wheel was not a problem; there were only two light steering chains to detach. But I was many miles from home, and even further from mechanical help.

Later, having spent the day making my rounds, I was ready to go home, but there was this little matter of the wheel-less tail. The repairs would have to be done at High Level. Rather than fly to the main airport and land on pavement I opted for the older grass strip adjacent to town. There was no problem landing; I just kept the tail up longer than usual. The grass did no damage to the tail as it slid to a halt. My mechanic looked after the problem from there.

Another incident at the High Level Airport was somewhat less painless. My annual inspection (Certificate of Airworthiness) having been completed, Luella and I drove in from LaCrete to recover the plane. It was Sunday and things were quiet when we arrived but there had obviously been some wild proceedings earlier. A Cessna 185 had gone on a rampage. Its destructive circuit was easily discernable in the skiff of snow.

When one of the pilots had gone to start his plane earlier, he had found his batteries dead. When you don't have a starter you start her by the prop. Our friend was too successful in his efforts. Had the brakes not been set? Who knows! Before the snow settled, that errant bird had torn into first one, then the second, and finally a third plane, coming to an overdue halt whittling at the innards of the third plane.

During this process, the vagrant chewed up the wing of one of the planes involved, tearing out an aileron counterweight. This weight was thrown high into the air, only to come straight down tearing two neat holes through the fabric of my wing, narrowly missing the gas tanks. We did not take home our plane after all.

Other incidents come to mind. In the month of March of our last year at Meander River, I wished to make one last visit to John D'Or Prairie and Fox Lake. By then I was not able to fly, being unable to pass my annual medical. I was relying on my Dodge pick-up. The plan was to spend Saturday at John D'Or, and Sunday at Fox Lake; but by late Saturday afternoon the thawing process had made the overland route, on the north side of the Peace River, between the two settlements difficult if not impossible. As I travelled toward home that night I decided I could spend the night in Fort Vermilion and then try for Fox Lake on Sunday, using the south road.

Sunday morning I had only a little food left, but I knew Fort wouldn't wake up for hours. Anyway, I could likely buy some chips and pop in Fox Lake, so I didn't even have breakfast.

The southern route involved the crossing of two ice bridges, one over the Wabasca, the other over the Little Red River. By that time the experience in the overflow on the Peace was a somewhat faded memory. Furthermore, I have an unfortunate tendency to believe that the things I want to do I should be able to do—even if a little extra effort might be required.

Thus, when I reached the Wabasca River and noticed frozen overflow I dared to believe a little extra speed might just enable the truck to crash through. I got through alright, through the ice which reached nicely to the bumper, insuring that I was going nowhere. This marked the beginning of a long day.

My resources were decidedly limited. No axe, one jackall, one extension cord, a plastic garbage bag, a rod-type jack-crank, a tow rope and two or three mud clods frozen into the approach on the river bank. My food supply consisted of a banana or two and not much else. To itemize the procedures of the next thirteen hours would exhaust all of us but the program was somewhat as follows:

Pray. Join truck and clod with the extension cord, jackall and tow rope. Put tension on the tow rope. Start truck and take stretch out of towrope. Repeat procedure. Don't dislodge clod. Repeat procedure many times. Notice front brakes are frozen. Remove wheels. Don't fall into water. Replace wheels. Repeat procedure.

Jackalls have been referred to as "widow makers" because of their dangerous tendencies. Not only are they inclined to slip, but their handles generate a lethal whip when the jack is loaded if the cogs begin to slip.

Trying to take the wheels off was awkward. Not only was the jack standing in water and on ice, but I had to work off of the ice in which the truck was caught. While I was thus laboriously engaged, the handle got away from me and started to whip. Fortunately it missed my head, especially in view of the fact that I was standing over water!

Having finally gained a few feet, I repeated the performance using the second clod. Meanwhile I froze a log into a rut using slush off the river. This log was to give me something to pull from when the clods broke away.

When I ran out of pull on the second clod I was just short of being able to reach the third one. What to do? Somehow the rod intended as a jack-crank, when straightened, furnished the missing link. Later I dismantled a "hazard" sign to lay under the wheels. It was of little help, it being about as slick as the ice. The garbage bag became a useful container which enabled me to carry dry dirt from the opposite side of the river. It was to furnish traction.

When the back wheels were finally out of the water the next

concern was to keep them there. I feared I might lose my hard-won gains. Whenever I gained a few inches I would, while at the steering wheel, work back, with a long stick, a log laid in front of a rear wheel. This was an awkward stunt, and I suspect that the pop I heard, while thus engaged, may have been my lower left rib cracking. Some day I should have it x-rayed, just for interest's sake.

If I was being successful it was by insignificant increments. After about twelve hours of relentless effort the back wheels were up on the bank but I still wasn't going anywhere fast , actually not even slowly. The ice and mud refused to allow the truck up the steep incline.

About ten thirty that night help arrived. Some equipment operators from LaCrete were on their way to a scarification project, likely planning to start work at midnight. Getting up on the roadway was no problem then.

The completeness of my relief was somewhat—but only somewhat—diminished by the realization that I was now free to begin my three or four hour trip home to Meander River. Nor was there to be a lunch or even coffee before High Level. By the time I reached Fort Vermilion the whole place was shut down again. (The people of Fort tend to be philosophical about working hours.)

Even if I could remain awake, the trip was not to be entirely incident-free. As I drove down Highway 58 at about 1:30^{am} I was dismayed to see flashing lights ahead. All I wanted to do was go home and get a few hours sleep before school. The last thing I needed was flashing lights!

As it turned out, several ladies from outside had been to the carnival at Fox Lake using the northern road. The road had been terrible, true to promise. But more than that, they had a flat about 25 miles back, and had been unable to remove the wheel. (They never explained to me why they stopped where they did.) Yes, I would give them a hand.

As it turned out, some zealot with an air-impact wrench, no doubt, had replaced the wheel. There was no way that I could turn the wheel nuts. One of the ladies was of the substantive sort, so even though it grieved me to have to rout her from the warm cab, I suggested she give me a hand (foot really). As she stood on one arm of that spanner wrench, I produced a dedicated effort on the matching cross member—with success.

No further memories involving the remainder of the trip registered. My brain was likely too dead. When I arrived in High Level someone had an Eatmore bar and a root beer waiting for me. The nap before school was highly condensed and exceedingly concentrated.

Arlyn had stopped by that weekend on his way south from Fort Chipewyan. I had left for school by the time he got up. He was baffled by the unusual gear in my pick-up, especially the bedraggled extension cord.

Since I was well past 45 by the time we moved to Meander River, I had to have an annual medical, in order to maintain my flying license. During that last visit I candidly shared with the M.O.T. examiner that I could, in fact, generate chest pains by running. I thought it was a logical state of affairs. Not he! The subsequent medical adventures left me wiser but still without the freedom to fly.

I would enjoy a little aerial jaunt, even today, but I console myself with the realization I was able to fly for 25 years more than most people, and that we had the plane when we really needed it.

My last flight, even as my first one, stands out rather clearly in my memory. Rev. Charlie Koop wanted to visit his parishioner, Arlyn, in Fort Chipewyan. Yes, I would take him.

Takeoff from Fort Vermilion Airport was not quite according to the book. A paving crew was at work on the regular runway, so we contented ourselves with a little trail in the grass beside the runway and got away. (Fortunately by next day the paving crew had moved on.)

During the night, a 40 knot gale blew east across the great delta and into Fort Chip. Why it didn't make off with ELC, I will never know! Likely the Lord understood that neither Charlie nor I enjoyed walking that much. (Airport builders can spend a million dollars building an airport but it never seems to occur to these people that planes should be tied down. A hand-me-down cable, tethered at intervals, is all that is required. Government, you know!)

Since our plane was still available to us in the morning we decided we might just as well use it. A weather warning had been issued to all marine craft, but we weren't marine. Fortunately, we could take off directly into the wind, fly into it the whole distance, and land directly into it at Fort Vermilion. I doubt that it would have been possible to land in a cross wind of that force.

Someone told me later that, upon his safe arrival home, Charlie reported he had prayed the whole time, except for ten minutes. Why the lapse? I'm not certain. Certainly the wind did not let up. I was relieved to wait out the storm before continuing to High Level.

That was my last flight! Just like that, one of life's chapters snaps shut!

Departures and arrivals from roadways sometimes seemed necessary, but were chancy. Once Arlyn needed a ride back into Fort Chip after spending time at a camp near Loon Lake. Rain had made the local strip, near Red Earth, difficult so we decided to use the road as the pick up spot.

After landing, I became aware of a power line just further down the road. It could have furnished a nasty surprise. The bush crowded the road from both sides, hiding the power poles which supported the line across the road. The line itself would have been difficult to see during an approach. Fortunately, I had gotten down on the road before reaching the line.

Chapter 24

Other Characters of Note

Meeting the many individualists who choose to live out in the remote regions is another significant benefit that comes to those who wander from the path that others beat. It is in the remote corners of the hinterland where these non-conformists are to be found. Do such people seek out obscure corners or do they become individualistic as they live isolated lives in their setting where they arrived for some other reason? Likely both factors are operative. Living in the outside world involves a certain amount of conformity. Some who refuse to be put into boxes end up in the boondocks, and because they tend to retain their individuality they have interesting accounts to relate. The general area which I worked from LaCrete had its share.

The non-conformist theory may explain why a butler of former times came to be our host when Bob Stanton and I made our unscheduled stop at the Trout Mountain fire tower. The stories he told us that Saturday night were entertaining, but I didn't get the impression he had any desire to relive his experiences any more realistically than as he was doing.

In another instance I was visiting an older gentleman when the conversation turned to the hover ferry that conveyed traffic across the Peace. Our family had been across the English Channel and the memory of a hovercraft was still fresh in my mind. Yet I hesitated to speak of the channel, Calais and the Cliffs of Dover, thinking such places were likely far removed from his experience. I need not have been concerned; when I mentioned that area, he came alive.

He had been a soldier overseas. Mention of Europe was all that was needed to open a host of memories. My new friend kept me entertained for hours relating experiences with great detail right down to how many bottles of beer had been drunk during a particular afternoon 40 years previous. His keen mind could certainly express itself.

This matter of self-expression has always been a source of

amazement to me. Even when the English employed by some of these backwoods spinners-of-yarn didn't originate in Oxford, the stories take shape very well. Maybe such people articulate so clearly because they observe keenly and remember minutely.

We explain the unusual artistic abilities of the Native people with a similar explanation. "Unusual" is not too strong a word. One Sunday, when I was out and about, I gave a ride to a hitch-hiker. Just what his affairs entailed I'm not certain. I suspect a certain amount of "hanky-panky." I believe the explanation offered was that his community was publishing a book of local artwork. He had with him about 30 large drawings, all well done; and each by a different artist. These drawings came out of a small community. To this day I keep some of the Native children's art work for appreciation. It is interesting that I should discover this transient and all the others of whom I write in this section, within 15 miles of one another.

About the time I was beginning to use the Peace River Airport, Peace Air Ltd. was getting under way. Peace Air did charter work as well as maintenance of their and others' planes.

When pilots had to wait for passengers whom they had brought to Little Buffalo, they would sometimes pass their time at our house. One of Peace Air's pilots whom we met in this fashion was Mike Papirny.

Years later I again visited with Mike but this time it was in his home at Keg River Cabins down the Mackenzie Highway. During that visit he told me the following amazing story. I will condense the account considerably. When he talked about this experience, he could give it in 'wave by wave' detail.

The event transpired on Great Bear Lake on the Arctic Circle where Mike was based at Trophy Lodge doing charter work for Peace Air using CF VZD. Ronald Austin, chief pilot for Atlantic Richfield Canada, David Smith, mechanic: and several geologists were also based at the lodge. Their plane was a Beaver, CF-ROC.

On August 1, 1970 Smith had kept a rendezvous with the geologists at Douglas Point, 90 miles from the lodge.

While the necessary tasks involving the geologists were being completed, ROC's batteries weakened to a point where they were unable to start the turbo engine. The geologists had a call for help relayed to the lodge. Papirny, taking a generator with him, set off at 11:30pm and arrived at Douglas Point at 12:45am.

Before ROC was ready for takeoff at 3:30am a great wind had risen. Because it threatened to smash both planes on the rocks, the decision to fly was made.

Austin and Smith went first in ROC. As they were taxiing across the bay seeking a sheltered area from which to take off, a line squall was seen heading in their direction. Rather than risk being swamped, Austin tried to take off.

The terrible force of wind and water was too great, causing the left float to rupture and crumple. As the left side of the plane sank into the five to seven foot swells, Austin quickly inflated his life jacket and jumped into the frigid waters. He was soon separated from the craft. Smith, a non-swimmer, managed to get out the right side and cling to a float.

Fortunately Papirny saw the spray created, and realized something of what had happened. Despite the mortal danger, Mike enlisted the help of the geologists who wrestled the Cessna 185 straight into the smashing waves away from the threatening rocks, so that he might try to effect a rescue. Two miles of rough water separated the parties. Progress was slow because extreme caution was required lest the propeller strike a wave.

While Papirny battled his way through the storm, the men in the water battled for their lives. The trip took about 30 minutes. Fortunately Papirny was able to spot Austin whom he then set about rescuing. Extreme care was required lest the waves cause Austin to be washed into the prop.

The first pass was unsuccessful. Papirny tried to throw a rope but the strong wind prevented Austin from grabbing it. Having made a second pass, Papirny got out on the float and extended an oar to Austin. By that time the 200 pound Austin was so paralysed by cold he was unable to heave himself out of the water. Fortunately, Papirny was able to grab him by the seat of his pants and haul him up onto the pitching float and into the cabin.

Restarting his engine, Papirny manoeuvred his plane downwind, crosswind, and into the swells in his attempt for the life of Smith. Fighting wind, waves and now heavy rain, Papirny had also to be cautious lest he become entangled in the overturned craft. Having approached as close as he dared, he ordered Smith to jump. Taking him literally, Smith made a feet first jump which landed him dangerously close to the propeller, but Papirny was able to swing the plane so the rear end of the right float came within reach. Papirny was then able to hoist Smith onto the float too.

Shortly thereafter ROC sank beneath the swells.

The takeoff was rough. A delayed nervous reaction brought on a case of nausea for Papirny. His seeking relief with a blast of cold air brought howls from the half-frozen passengers. Poor visibility and heavy weather necessitated an indirect flight to the lodge.

Upon reaching Trophy Lodge at 5:55am the two fortunate survivors were treated to a roaring fireplace, and a circulation-restoring rub-down with warm bath towels. Meanwhile, Papirny returned to Douglas Bay for the geologists.

For this selfless, heroic and skilful rescue Papirny received many recognitions and awards. On January 5, 1971 Lt. Governor Grant MacEwan awarded him the Life of Alberta Gold Medal. On June 22, 1973 Governor General Michener, on behalf of the Queen, presented him with the Star of Courage. These would be the most prestigious of the awards received. Although Mr. Papirny was retired by 1998, he still flew his own plane maintaining his commercial license.

At another time I was rewarded for my efforts to get out and around because I was thus enabled to meet Harry Bows. His memory also deserves to be kept alive.

Now Harry's dwelling was unique. I mention it first because it was his home that first caught my attention. It was the type of place where I had to remind myself I was not a curious tourist. Eye control was of importance. The purpose of such visits was to see people, not places. I did not go about prying into other people's lives and I did not want to leave the impression that was my intent. Harry's was one of the last places I was going to stop in Keg River Post that Sunday.

During subsequent visits I usually arranged to stop at his place last, because by that time it would be dark and I was prepared to relax over a plate of his mulligan stew while listening to a few more stories.

Harry, too, had been a soldier in the First World War. His had been the task of getting behind the enemy lines with a radio set to report to his buddies how things like shelling appeared to be going from that perspective. During his time of service he was deafened—totally, I believe. Much later he was walking along beside a train in some railway station when, without explanation, his hearing came back.

In civilian life Harry filled many roles as a pioneer in the Keg River Post Area. His name appears frequently in Frank Jackson's two books relating to that area. When I got to know him, he was tending the weather equipment for his region. Among other things he had been a surveyor, a telephone line maintenance man and farmer. Harry had a wealth of stories.

I would have liked to have been with him at the time of his death but I was a little too late. At noon that day, I received a message at school in LaCrete from one of Harry's neighbours that his end was near. I did not like to leave my classroom but I determined to fly to Manning immediately after school to see him. A total stranger at Grimm's service station near the airfield let me borrow his pick-up to go to the hospital. I lost no time, but when I got to Harry's bedside, the sheet was already pulled up over his face.

Also at Keg River Post, it was my pleasure to meet both Frank and Dr. Mary Jackson, two other notable pioneers of that area. I can hardly begin to tell Dr. Jackson's story other than to introduce her as a young British doctor who, upon learning of Alberta's needs, opted for a career in Alberta rather than India.

She chose to serve in a part of the world where, almost like India, doctors were almost unheard of. Her strenuous, self-sacrificing and skilful efforts were greatly appreciated. Her "hospital" was the vast region north of Peace River Crossing; her clients were the needy among both the natives and whites (including LaCreters); her duties were as varied as the needs she met; and her rewards were mostly the gratitude of a people who realized something of the magnitude of her contribution.

In time she married the widower Frank Jackson who had stories of his own to relate.

Mary was afforded many honours but the one she shared with her husband was one given by the Government of Alberta in the 1950's—The Farm Family of the Year Award.

Mary's story is told by Cornelia Lehn in the book, *The Homemade Brass Plate,* printed by Fraser Valley Custom Printers, Chilliwack, B.C.

Mr. Jackson's stories were written as he told them to Sheila Douglas. These softcover books go under the titles, *A Candle in the Grub Box,* and its sequel, *Jam in the Bed Roll.* They were published by Shires Books, 246 Seafield Rd., Victoria, B.C. V9S 1S6.

Chapter 25

We Pull Up Tent Stakes

During our thirteenth year at LaCrete, a period of change began. We did not realize the significance of events as they unfolded, but as I review them a pattern emerges. By 1986 there were changes on the teaching scene, in my farming affairs, in the real estate area and in our family matters.

Where our children were concerned, our big LaCrete house had lost some of its significance. Arlyn was church planting in Fort Chipewyan on the other side of hundreds of miles of bush. Laurella was in nurse's training in Red Deer. Lyndell was attending Moody Bible Institute in Chicago preparing for a career in avionics. Lanna-Marie was preparing to leave home to take Grade 10 at Prairie High School in Three Hills. Home was going to be different!

With the boys gone, my fooling at farming made even less sense than it had. Driving a tractor up and down a field had lost any excitement. One evening I was out disking some new breaking next to the lake when a problem developed. After picking up the disk I bounced toward home across the rough ground. As the disk jerked about, the draw-pin bounced out. Upon glancing behind I noticed the disk sitting well back, with two rubber bands, which used to be hydraulic hoses, stretched between it and the tractor. I looked around just in time to get a bath in hydraulic fluid. I had suddenly finished farming at LaCrete!

The time was not yet ten o'clock, early by LaCrete standards; there was time to pay my near neighbour, Mr. Braun, a visit. Yes, he would be interested in renting my land. We agreed on a share crop basis, but we found a written agreement unnecessary. When Mr. Braun retired from farming, his sons took over and continue to work my land. Several times a year they send along a reminder that the land still produces. In a world of legalities, lawsuits and lawyers it is a pleasure to deal with people whose word is their bond.

If I wasn't going to farm, there would be no need for machinery. Next morning was Saturday, sale day at the Auction Mart, so at six o'clock, when Luella got up and looked out the window, she was surprised to see a whole string of machinery in the yard. I moved what I could to the Auction Mart before the sale started at 10 o'clock. The rest had to wait. Proceeds were not overwhelming, but did pay for our visit to the World Exposition being held in Vancouver that summer.

Changes were transpiring on the teaching scene as well. After 12 years of teaching mostly Junior High in LaCrete, the thought of teaching adults appealed to me. Adult education involved a shorter year which allowed more time for my extra projects. Fairview College did adult work at LaCrete, but the Fort Vermilion School Division, my employer, was also thinking of entering the adult field.

When they approached me regarding teaching adults at Buffalo Head Prairie I agreed to do so. That September I spent most of my time preparing a program of studies. Classes were to begin in October.

There were interested students, but there was no financial help for them. Crops hadn't been the best, and bush work beckoned. The consequence was that only a few people participated, but we carried on until Christmas.

While I was spending my time with only several students, the Grade 5–6 teacher was overloaded with a class of 36 youngsters. There seemed to be ample justification for splitting the 5–6 class and giving me Grade 6. This is how we began the new year. I continued to put some effort into supervising the several adults who continued, but it was obvious the children had to receive most of the attention.

My real estate matters were also evolving. We had added the NW quarter of section 9 to our holdings. It was kitty-corner to the LaCrete town-site then still situated, for the most part, on SE of 9. The potential for development was there, but there were some seemingly insurmountable hurdles. How would one begin?

During the time period under discussion another opportunity presented itself. Uranium City on the north shore of Lake Athabasca had been deserted by all but 100 people. The uranium mine, which had been its reason for being, had been shut down by the government without warning. The associated jobs were gone, but many fine buildings remained.

By the time I learned of this, many of the homes had been moved out. The houses which were too wide to go south over the narrow bush roads had been barged to points along the Athabasca System. The mobile homes and double-wides had been moved overland to Meadow Lake, Saskatchewan. Even so there were many fine, and more not-so-fine, houses left.

A moving program looked feasible. My intention was to have these houses barged down Lake Athabasca, down the Quatre Fourche River, up the Peace River and finally we would move them overland to wherever a house might be needed.

One of the customers I hoped to entice was the Fort Vermilion School Division which needed about seven teacherages at the time. Since they could not deal with me as long as I was an employee, I thought it best to alter that status. Thus I resigned my Grade 6 position in Buffalo Head Prairie as of May 31,1986.

Unfortunately, after I flew one of their officials to Uranium City, the Division was still not interested in my proposal.

I completed the school term as a substitute teacher in my own classroom, so things seemed fairly normal during that summer. The truth of the matter was that I had no job, nor did Luella at the time.

One day, as I was busily stuffing insulation into the rafters of the large addition which we were building onto our church, the Deputy Superintendent of the Fort Vermilion School Division drove into the yard. Would we like to teach in Meander River?

Having very positive memories about teaching Native children, both Luella and I were happy to accept the Meander positions. There were just the two of us then. So off we toodled down the MacKenzie Highway to our new home and tasks in Meander River 40 miles north of High Level and about one hour short of the North West Territories. Thus began the next seven year period of our lives.

Chapter 26

Our Meander Years

The Meander experience bore little resemblance to what we had lived at Little Buffalo. The children likewise had good tans, but that was where the similarities ended. Certainly the lives which we lived there were unique and merit a chapter or two in this chronicle.

Upon our arrival at Meander River we found the setting pleasant and picturesque. Our home and the school were adequate. Most of the settlement rested on the high banks of the Hay River, but on the lower flats, near the confluence of the Hay and Meander Rivers, rested the remainder of the settlement. The serenity of this scene belied the storms that unsettled the school's interior. Both Luella and I completed our teaching careers in this environment, Luella by teaching mostly Special Education, while I worked with Grades 4–6. High Level was our town during those years. It was where we did most of our business and where we went to church.

Where the community was concerned, we apparently were not needed. A good paved road put the people within easy reach of the services offered in High Level. At Little Buffalo it was a given that teachers would visit homes and be a part of life in general, but at Meander people seemed quite unused to having teachers involved in the community beyond school.

Life in the school was totally unlike anything we had experienced. Hopefully we did not have any inflated and high-blown designs for the place, for the children had no aspirations that would have seemed to coincide! It became apparent that if we were going to enjoy any authority and respect, we were going to have to earn them.

Part of the problem was that, of the 11 members of the teaching staff, only John Balfour had taught there previously. He had gained respect and status, but as for the rest of us—who did we think we were to walk into the children's lives and start dictating? During a future summer we came to understand more fully the children's position.

All through the school year the children are expected to obey, respect and appreciate their teacher. He in his turn is expected to be a friend to his students. Hopefully this bonding will take place and often it does. Ironically, the more thorough the bonding, the deeper the wound when the teacher packs up and leaves at the end of the year—with never a backward look. This is the children's experience year after year. Can they be blamed for resenting another intrusion? The person whom the children regarded as a friend proves to be just another opportunist who played with their hearts!

This process is less obvious in most schools, but in remote schools it is another matter. In a place like Meander River, the school is the centre of children's lives, where they play with friends, are occupied during the school day, are fed lunches and, most importantly, engage in sports activities. In a village without strong families or a strong economy, when the school shuts down, there's not much left.

As our first year wore on, things settled. In time we gained a degree of respect and authority.

A large factor in our Meander experience was the paved MacKenzie Highway beside which we lived. This allowed daily mail deliveries and town-type services within 45 minutes. A doctor would visit once a week. Otherwise people could readily go to the medical services offered in High Level. We were never approached to offer this type of assistance. All in all we were more a part of normal life.

Some accommodation was provided near the school. We lived in a comfortable bungalow. There was also a triplex next door. Most of the teachers preferred to jointly commute from High Level.

One year the triplex was occupied by our good friend, Ronan McDonald, Carolyn Stoddart and an adult education teacher. Carolyn will likely never tell this story, so I might as well. By this particular Saturday night the Adult Education teacher had moved out, but had not locked his windows. Ronan was in High Level. Arlyn (who was visiting) and I were loading his truck at about 1:30am when Luella received a phone call from Carolyn, would I come and get her? Our doors were separated by about 50 feet. When I got to her door the poor girl was terrified. Having flu at the time, she had taken medication and gone into a deep sleep. Suddenly she awoke to see a face looking at her from under a trap door in her floor. One of the local lads had come calling via the adult teacher's suite. He had made his way through the crawl space under the three suites and decided to surface right next to Carolyn's bed. By the time Luella and I returned from church later that day, Carolyn was half moved to High Level. My guess is that she now checks every new apartment for trap doors.

Over the years a vast change had occurred in the educational system. Salaries bore little relation to the $1900 per year that had been my starting wage. The old gelatin pan hectograph (which incidentally I never did master) had been replaced by a sophisticated multi-colour photocopier. There was a school secretary and enough aides to give us adequate help. Class sizes were small—nothing like the 28 children in eight grades which I had during my first years of teaching or the 35 children in one grade later.

Yet, even with all of these pluses, I cannot describe the task as easy. It was not, for there has been a change in the children, too, largely due to a damaged environment in the home. Likely most of that unfortunate change must be due to the debilitating and powerful influence of TV.

During the 19 years that we lived in Native communities we always made a point of visiting the homes. Sometimes the people were a little shy when we came to their cabins. For us these visits offered some lessons. What love and unity there was in most of those families, what peace and quiet in the pre-TV days! The homes in many cases were models of serenity.

Unfortunately, much of that has changed. The snug log cabins have been replaced with drab, echoing frame houses in which I rarely feel comfortable. Nor does that inevitable TV, invariably on to spoil any attempt at conversation, contribute anything positive.

If TV is a curse among white society it is doubly so among the Natives. How pathetic to see a once capable and productive man sitting idly and forlornly before a wretched tube passively drinking in the banality of over-paid actors emulating adulterers and fools.

Even though some effort is made to portray the minority groups, albeit inaccurately, of the western world, most of what appears on the screen is "White." If the White viewer has any capacity for independent thought, he can filter what he sees through his experience and knowledge, thus avoiding some of the brain-washing process. The experiences of many Natives in the outside world are limited. When TV preaches its world view and morality as convincingly as it does, Indians especially, assume that is "the way it is."

How unfortunate that the positive effects of White life take root so much more reluctantly than do the destructive influences! This fact goes well beyond the television. Other pertinent examples are bingo, junk-food, drugs, tobacco, dirty politics, seedy music, and of course, the overwhelming scourge of booze!

Until my Meander days, I had always stressed academics. My policy was to cram as much math, science and English into the students as I could. In my opinion adult grade-school education is a stop-gap measure best avoided. Children have the time and capacity to learn. Most things they learn will come in handy sooner or later. On the other hand, major gaps left in their understanding and knowledge tend to haunt them in later years. Calculators, spell-checks, and grammar checks are poor substitutes for head knowledge.

Before long, in Meander, I realized that my educational philosophy and teaching habits would have to undergo modification.

Creativity was an area where I bent most. Art projects were still normally a pain. Suitable projects were difficult to originate and execute. In time I went for fewer, but larger and more complicated creations. One such effort was a wire-ribbed dragon about 20 feet long. It was a glorified timeline we used to depict the amazing succession of achievements of the Chinese people.

Later we got into fake taxidermy. Our creations included buffalo and moose heads as well as mountain sheep. I put a great deal of effort into the sheep. Having discovered that creating a matched pair of horns was beyond my ability, I persuaded the wildlife people in Edmonton to let me make a mold using a pair of their mountain sheep horns. Then I obtained a styrofoam head from a taxidermist supply place. Using these properly shaped items I prepared molds out of fibreglass. These molds were then used to contain polyurethane to create prototypes. A fake fur covering for the head, helped to create a natural effect.

Part of my reason for putting so much effort into this sheep was that I hoped it might have some commercial potential for the larger community. It was a forlorn and misplaced hope. The world was changing. On one hand, hunting and trapping activities were being increasingly frowned on. On the other hand, government policies being what they are, people had less and less incentive to put any effort at all into gainful employment.

Another classroom project involved the building of an airplane. This creation was patterned somewhat after my Cessna 140, and was about 3/4 the size. It hung from our classroom ceiling on three pulleys. When we wished to work on it we lowered it. There was no way of getting our project out of the classroom but I'm certain it would have flown as a glider, had we been able to take it outdoors.

Then there was the five foot windmill which looked akin to a waterwheel. It would not have fared well in a watery setting—constructed, as it was, of cardboard—so we powered it with cooling fans. The wheel in its turn spun three large cardboard boxes connected in tandem by a system of belts. The boxes, as they rotated, were ideal for portraying such themes as the passing of seasons, cartoons, or Christmas scenes.

I had as much fun building this stuff as the kids did.

There were numerous gadgets associated with science themes: a shoebox camera, an x-ray machine, a water production unit (We really wowed them with that one when we set it up in the hall at recess.), a circuit board, etc. The circuit board lit up when a bird's picture was properly matched, using wires, with its name. We also created a Rube-Goldberg device for popping balloons.

Of all our creations I consider our last one to have been our best. Likely it could be best described as a carousel. This machine grew from a large plywood disk suspended from the high ceiling by a shaft mounted on a car wheel hub. Protruding from this disk were eight arms, each about ten feet long. At the end of each arm was a little paper convertible about four feet in length. Each car was driven by a little bear. The bear was mostly head - a painted and decorated balloon about 16" in diameter.

The centre of the machine was a large cardboard barrel decorated with cellulose butterflies lit by an interior spotlight. The arms were also butterfly decorated. An electric motor caused the whole apparatus to slowly rotate. As the carousel majestically turned, a tape played merry-go-round music.

I guess you could say this was my "last hurrah." I was sorry to learn it was dismantled after I left. Later the whole school was replaced so the plane must have gone too.

One of the joys in creating these things was seeing, the boys especially, become more used to working with their hands, and for that matter, more willing. These large projects were the official ones. We spent other happy hours in the wood-working shop. One of the preferred items for individual construction was the pistol.

Another area which received an increased amount of attention during our Meander years was the field trip. Within a radius of 125 miles we had all manner of unfamiliar and interesting places and activities to visit. For instance, there was the buffalo ranch near Beaver Ranch and a regular community pasture near Fort Vermilion. The kids weren't the only ones to learn about pregnancy testing the day we visited the community pasture.

The Sam Boeses not only let us visit their cattle operation, but also fed us all lunch. On Mr. Teichroeb's farm at LaCrete he showed us how to make puffed wheat. He pressurized wheat in a pressure vessel by heating it. When he popped the lid the wheat puffed and blew into a cage.

Jake Fehr gave us the tour of their logging camp. Henry H. Peters showed us the LaCrete Pioneer village. Peter Giesbrecht taught us important things about farming equipment including, "No, the government didn't give it to me."

There were other field trips: to the Northwest Territories, to Edmonton and to Grande Prairie. One of the last took us to

Kananaskis where a University-sponsored program was offered to many Grade 6 groups. Although some aspects of the program were good, the main emphasis seemed to be the promotion of New Age concepts. I was disturbed by a woeful lack of understanding of the workings of nature among these would-be-teachers of nature. For instance, there were leaners in the trees where the children were spending a lot of their time. These fallen trees hanging in standing trees were just waiting to crash onto some unsuspecting child's head. I was told to leave them; they were natural. Well, they were a lot less natural shortly after the instructor turned his head! Surely one's stupidity must have some bounds!

This outing also involved skiing, swimming, and sessions at the Bennett Dam, the Calgary Tower, and West Edmonton Mall.

One of the more advantageous spin-offs of the Uranium City house idea was that I acquired a Class 1 driver's license in anticipation of driving large moving trucks. Thus I could do a lot of the bus driving myself. Most of the time Al took us. He was good with the children, and a reliable driver.

Although I was an active participant in these activities, and frequently the initiator, it was with a sense of unease. There was no doubt in my mind about the educational value of field trips, but it was the incidental learnings that gave me pause. Even after we had been out for days, the children would still come back to the bus, after another of our many gas stops, loaded with goodies and pop. One had to wonder how much money they had set out with. We had likely suggested $20 to be adequate. Were we not promoting careless spending habits? How will it be, if and when the well goes dry? I wanted the children to have a good time but were we creating in them expectations which might in future be impossible to meet?

(By comparison, when my own children had gone out for the day they were fortunate to have $3 to spend. Today they have respect for their earnings.)

Yes, there was injustice involved in the coming of the Europeans and in their establishing themselves on lands which the Indians roamed, but it should be remembered that in the process that followed the fruits of that land were released. Where it formerly supported few people at a subsistence level, during modern times, it supports many in comfort.

To those who argue that the White Man stole the land I say, "And if that is not bad enough, shall we now go on to rob him of his dignity, self-worth, and independence as well?"

Earlier I mentioned that hope is a vital ingredient in the human system of wellbeing. Hope's partner is planning. When a person has a dream, he likes to invest in it. If I plan to buy a new 4x4 I will have to sell a calf crop; but then I must have cows; they require a fence and hay; so I must break ground and plant grass and pray the stuff will grow. Next I had better have my tractor and baler ready during that precious week of baling weather so that I will be able to feed my cows that will produce the calves that will give me my 4x4.

We should all be concerned when the talents that could be used to build the fences, cut wood, draw pictures, cook meals, nurse the sick, run computers and repair cars lie latent. How can our nation absorb such waste? Last summer I was able to build a beautiful pine floor. Why? Because some latent pine seeds had sprung to life, borne fruit and given me their potential. And we should never be lulled into complacency by the idea that there seem to be many others to take up my slack. That is not how it works.

May Heaven help us when the United Nations starts intervening in our national affairs by pealing back the cocoon. Someone once noticed a butterfly having a bad time as it tried to free itself from the confines of its cocoon. Being kind and compassionate, he thought he would help. He tore away the restraining fibres and freed the grateful insect. But what sadness! What should have become a beautiful creature of the wild, remained a miserable representation of what might have been!

Mankind is not that different. God once wrote "in stone" that man was to become strong as he put effort into life. When we try to rewrite God's rule book, we invariably run into problems. Did anyone ever win, even a bronze medal, by training in bed?

Somehow, sometime soon, Canadians are going to have to understand we are not above the rules and restraints the rest of the world functions under.

The hour is late but not too late. A system that is just for all must yet be employed. If we appreciate our Aboriginal friends, we will cause our dealings with them to be determined by an understanding of what is required for their long-term good—and ours. Incidentally, rather than being mutually exclusive, as some would have us believe, our "goods" are very closely interwoven.

The scene needs statesmen, both Aboriginal and White; people of vision, compassion, insight and courage; people who cannot be dissuaded from the right course by the sentimental bleating of interest groups or by the prospect of a generous ballot box. Such leaders must have clear eyes and deaf ears—ears deaf particularly to the anguished cries of guilt-ridden, uninformed white society. They must recognize that wise decisions do not emanate from a cauldron seething with emotion and fired by avarice and guilt mongering.

Too long has the whole Indian and Northern Affairs bureaucracy, together with its political cronies, been burgeoning like cancer destroying the life which is purportedly being promoted. Too long have threats of such evils as cultural "genocide" been used as clubs to beat into submission the bureaucrats' detractors. Much of what is being done is under the guise of generosity, compassion, and good will, plus a truckload of related sentiment, but the consequences (and these are only just beginning to emerge) of this perverse generosity are anything but benevolent. Where are the cattle, the grain crops, the gardens, the mines, the factories and even the lumber mills that produce real wealth? And I might add, the trappers and wood piles. Even trapping, which was once a source of pride and relative prosperity, has been taken from them.

In 1998 I generated about 70 dollars of revenue for Ottawa for every dollar the treasury sent me. Yet, even though I will be 67 next Monday, I do not feel it is beneath me to go to the bush and get firewood to heat our home. Should it be unthinkable that other younger people should also go out into fire-killed areas to harvest beautiful firewood instead of burning expensive and often hard-to-get propane? Certainly a lack of equipment should not pose a problem.

Think how proud the children who are growing up without a

work ethic would be to see Dad haul in a load of firewood that he made with his own hands! It would be even more helpful if the children were obliged to help in the process. Any time a boy grows to manhood without ever having been forced to work and succeed, he has a real problem developing self-confidence and self-respect. For an unbelievable number of them suicide is the direct result. Would it ever occur to anyone in the system to replace their guidance counsellors whispering soft platitudes about self-worth and self-esteem and self this and that with a caring father carrying a chainsaw? He might not have a degree behind his name, but nature could provide him with about 30 of the negative variety to help him make his points.

Many are growing up undisciplined, unable to understand the concept of "no." Many have little understanding of economic concepts. For instance, the idea that someone has to earn what others are given to spend is a startling revelation. My little friends at Meander became quite indignant when they learned that Mother Ottawa deducted income tax from my pay-cheque!

Multiculturalism with its handmaidens, isolationism and ghettoisation spawn a venomous brood. Its promotion is a short-sighted method of producing long term woes. Surely Canada's present pangs of disintegration involving Quebec are as graphic an example of what comes of fractured Canadianism as anyone should need. I submit that if the Plains of Abraham had been followed up with a one-nation, one-people policy we would not now be having today's problems. Yes, to have followed that course at that time would have seemed cruel, but there are few things as cruel as civil war even though it be deferred for a century or two.

When different cultures are put together, there is likely to be friction. But when the static electricity produced is dispersed as it builds, an explosion is averted. On the other hand, when the intermingling is artificial and limited, the charge builds to dangerous levels.

These principles hold true in the school scene as well as in the larger world. Earlier we mentioned the Northland School Division, my employer for 12 years. This Division was designed to meet the needs of a particular people group. Not only was it a cumbersome and expensive operation to run, but the very principles on which it was founded were faulty. They, by their very nature were divisive, promoting isolationism.

In the Fort Vermilion School Division, my employer for 20 years, a superior system was in place. Schools meeting the needs of a vast spectrum of religious and ethnic groups tended to bring the people together. The teachers mingled, as did the children from diverse villages, particularly in sports.

Yes, there were unpleasant occurrences, but the worst of them had more to do with origin of community than with origin of blood. The shots that were fired were across a net or into a goal and drew no blood. Who could be faulted for drubbing the enemy in a game of volley ball? All the time such shots were being fired they produced mutual respect and admiration. Can there be racial strife when there is mutual respect?

Another area in which this mingling was very helpful was in the matter of scholastics.

In a school setting, isolationism allows teachers and students to lose sight of what is possible if, in fact, they were ever aware of what is possible. They are apt, in a secluded environment, to settle for the comfortable. Unchallenged students may be comfortable students, but they will be underachievers. The cumulative consequence of having the educational system pander to underachievers is that the unchallenged discover too late that the boat has left. Overcoming the problem of a defective education is very difficult during adult life, and likely impossible. Adult education is not the answer.

One of the reasons why astounding levels of achievement are reached at the Olympics is because the bar is way up there and people come forward from all over the earth to challenge it. If the residents of a ghetto place the bar, seeming success is easier to obtain, but when the sheltered leave their secure environment they will likely suffer a debilitating shock from which they may never recover.

For years I wondered about the Canadian psyche. We saw ourselves as a great and generous people—the originators of Medicare, peace keepers to the world, compassionate, crime- free, and generally superior to our gun toting, drug using, poverty tolerant, medicare-less neighbours to the south. Finally the answer came to me. I remembered the muskrat and beaver pelts that came in with great slash-induced scars. The trappers explained that when the animals have lots of space and good food they do not abuse one another, but when things become tight, the animals attack one another, vying for limited resources.

We of Canada have become used to our great spaces, our vast resources, and our generally favourable circumstances. More than used to them, we feel these benefits are our ordained rights! It never occurs to our minds that to us have been extended gifts as a trust to be carefully maintained. We have been very casual about "keeping our fences maintained and the roofs shingled," carelessly assuming that what is, will ever be.

Have we stopped to consider, for instance, that the harsh Canadian environment, which was largely instrumental in shaping us as a capable and self-reliant people, might yet turn devastatingly upon us?

We have mortgaged three generations' worth of houses through irresponsible spending. What is to come of our much praised social net if the loan is suddenly called? A tin roof, a bowl of rice and pair of short pants hardly meet the requirements of a harsh Canadian winter!

Even so, we learn so poorly. At the time of writing, the federal government has managed to gouge the longsuffering Canadian taxpayer to the point where there was actually to be a surplus of some five billion dollars. Did they use it to pay down our almost 600 billion dollar debt? No, this money was thrown about at this or that interest group. Had even that five billion been used to pay down the debt, at 8% interest per annum, 400 million dollars per year might have been saved.

What makes Canadians and particularly the people in Ottawa, think we can defy the most elementary standards of common sense without serious consequence?

Of the assortment of memories we brought with us from Meander River, possibly the most vivid are those that have to do with their frequent funerals. Earlier I wrote of the close ties that bind many of the Native communities. It was during those unfortunate but frequent times of bereavement that the bonds became most apparent. During our years at Little Buffalo, the people had a strength of character drawn from a way of life, not yet totally disrupted, but close to nature. There were few deaths. As time went on, this changed in all of the communities with which we were associated. Death and grief seemed ever present.

During our years at Meander, we were hardly out of one heart-wrenching situation before we were plunged into another. I won't intrude into the people's privacy to even try to communicate the grief, anguish, despair and hopelessness. We tried to share their grief but we knew that we had no real comprehension.

We attended their wakes and funerals. These were very important aspects of the mourning process. No effort was spared to make things as nice as possible but flowers can't heal broken hearts. They may soothe the pain somewhat.

I used to wish they would not be so hard on themselves. During the nights the body was available before the funeral, it was usually kept in the home. All night, people would stay with the body. Nor were there but a few. It seemed everyone would come to sit, visit, eat and smoke. The house would be packed. How very tiring! Or did I miss something? Was it from the crowd that the bereaved gathered strength?

Collegues from La Crete, Meander River, Fort Vermilion and High Level organized a surprise send-off for Henry Enns.

I'll miss your hardy hellos in the morning. I hope you have a fun filled life. Take Care! Anne

"Don't Worry Be Happy" Enjoy your Freedom. Ta[illegible] Brother

May you be blessed for all the things you've accomplished and enjoy your Golden Years Fern

Best of luck in your retirement, Henry! I enjoyed our tête a têtes. L. Belech[illegible]

Henry, It has been a pleasure having a colleague such as yourself! All the best! Rhonda

Have a wonderful time in Meadow Lake. We'll be thinking about you regularly Jan

What can we [illegible] besides that we [illegible] all miss you around the [illegible] Nobody to whistle in the halls at recess time. No more new carousels or airplanes. Will we ever invent anything again. Anne

Good luck to your new home and take care. I wish you could have at least stayed one more year. Thank you for everything. Dean-na Salopree.

HENRY, YOU ARE LEAVING SOME VERY BIG MOCCASINES/ COWBOY BOOTS TO FILL. HOPE I PICKED UP A THING OR TWO FROM THE "S T O R I E S".

THE MAN,
THE LEGEND,
THE STORY:

I AM WAITING FOR THE MOVIE TO HIT THE BIG SCREEN. THANKS FOR ALL YOUR HELP + ADVICE

ALL THE BEST WITH FUTURE SCAMS RJ.

GOOD-BYE!
WE'LL MISS YOU!

Thanks for getting my truck unstuck and for just being there.
Maureen

Thank you for answering questions and rescuing me!
Carolyn

...ve known you ...r seven long years. Take it ...sy, don't over work yourself in Meadow Lake...
Doint

Good Luck Mr Enns.
God bless you and Mrs Enns in good Health. you will be in our thought.
will miss you.
Lry

Gonna miss you, Mr. Enns. It was a pleasure having you here! Good luck!
Angelique

Early property development activities of Vangard

Chapter 27

The Vangard Realty, Ltd. Chapter

Recognizing that accounts of construction activities interest some readers less than others, I considered moving this segment to the appendix, but because Vangard is such an integral part of my life, I will dare to put it here.

During the spring of 1993 I had a strong sense that my total of 38 years in the classroom was about right for me. My voice was tired. My poor hearing made communication with the children difficult. Luella's brother, 20 hours away, was dying. Her mother, 15 hours away had Alzheimers. Luella had already been retired for two years. The time had come to close the teaching chapters of my life. If circumstances were otherwise, I could still enjoy teaching, but one of the situations that I wished to avoid was that of a "has been" forcing himself on children.

As for other challenges, I did not have far to search. Vangard Realty Ltd. had become a project of opportunity and potential. It offered ample scope for any of my capacities that still existed.

While my teaching career was winding down in Meander River, the land development process was getting underway in LaCrete. Because I am often asked about my company, something of its history and activities would seem to fit here.

When the name, Vangard Realty, comes up it should not bring to mind images of apartment complexes and office towers. Vangard's activities are related to the development and sale of lots. The buildings from Pine Point and Uranium City never became part of the operation. Nor should a staff of executives and secretaries be visualized. The President simply switches hats, or tries to wear several at the same time. Don't look for him in a three-piece suit presiding over a business lunch. If you wish to find him, look for a white hat and a well tanned, sweating back bending over a shovel. He may be a little grimy, but being careful to stay clean takes time. Or you may find him on-the-fly looking for another piece of equipment, a load of bedding sand or a batch of ready-mix concrete.

When he is not directly involved in construction he's likely at his desk or telephone or fax or calculator computing how much G.S.T. to ship east. Vangard must cause some joy in the halls of SaskTel when they enumerate those dozens and dozens of calls every month.

The binder entitled "Phase II A" is dated 1989. That first phase has been followed by 14 others. The sixteenth is presently underway. It is to undergo construction in May or June, 1999. Hopefully that work will not conflict with the trail ride we are planning.

My real estate career began during our Little Buffalo years when I purchased a large three-storey rooming-house in Peace River. This fine old building, complete with stained glass windows, had once belonged to the Hudson's Bay Company. It had been, in its youth, the factor's residence. The Bay must have gone to some effort to accommodate their staff.

This house was too large to be feasibly rented as a family dwelling so Mrs. Krause ran it as a rooming house. Before selling it I salvaged quite a number of items of antique furniture—even a deer trophy. Lyndell and I restored several pieces of furniture. These help furnish the house in which we live.

After we moved north, I opened bushland at LaCrete, Tompkins Landing, and Beaver Ranch. I was a teacher then doubling as a student in the school of "Hard Knocks." I graduated, both poorer and wiser.

In 1985 we bought most of our neighbour, Mrs. Fehr's, quarter. This was NW of 9, Township 106, Range 15 west of the 5th Meridian. Abe Harder had already done a small subdivision on that quarter. As other developers became disenchanted with the process, I bought their properties and developed them.

In development, location is the overriding consideration. The 16 acres Peter Teichroeb sold me were the key to the construction aspect and the future of Vangard. This parcel gave me the access I needed to develop the Fehr quarter.

Because the Company has acquired and developed various properties, it offers lots for a variety of purposes. We have for sale: house and mobile home lots, multi-dwelling and business lots.

Most of our customers are young families looking for a toehold, and Vangard offers easy terms. Some raise their eyebrows when they learn how easy, but no one has yet been reduced to starvation in the process.

Another favourite question is, "Why do you bother? You're supposed to be retired." I could ask, "Why does the guy climb a mountain?" Yes, I'm retired—from teaching. Likely the answer to the first question lies somewhere in the understanding of my personality. All my life I have worked hard. Work is a way of life for me. Although I can enjoy a game of golf, a few ends of curling, a session of windsurfing or a number of other activities, my problem is that before the session is half over, I am wondering if there are not some tasks I should be working at. I am still most content when I am building something, be it a barn, a wagon or a road.

Furthermore, work is my defence mechanism. TV and my sanity are incompatible. If I can get through a biased newscast without feeling inclined to sound off in the presence of my longsuffering wife, I feel I've been relatively successful. Then too, seeing wealth and prosperity being produced gives me pleasure. If the loonies are going into someone else's trousers, that is fine, just so long as our nation is being productive. And if no one else needs any spare bucks, certainly Mr. Chretien and his crony, Paul Martin, seem to need a lot. The truth of the matter is that there are many people who need financial help. Dozens of requests beg for responses.

Then, if I am going to complain about others living at public expense, consistency would suggest that I remain independent as long as possible. I feel it is to my credit and Ottawa's shame if they feel they must collect, through me, 73 cents for every penny of Old Age Pension they send me!

Not least of all, though, I gain a great deal of satisfaction from going through whole areas of town realizing that it was I who provided others with an opportunity to establish those homes. Of course, my customers paid their way, but even so, someone was required to get the lots in place and it does not necessarily follow that the task would have been done just because a need developed.

Several individuals and companies have been vital ingredients in Vangard's success. Two people should likely be mentioned. George Zacharias has sold more lots than the rest of us put together. He has been a good helper also in construction.

Peter F. Peters has been a great help with the year's-end requirements as well as in writing agreements and dealing with Land Titles. Unfortunately he has little energy left for these activities as he engages in his battle with cancer.

The helpful efforts of Knelsen Sand and Gravel have been mentioned elsewhere. Too many times have we at some unheard of hour needed concrete to cement a valve, thrust-block, "T" or fire hydrant. We always hesitate to turn off water for part of the town, so we sometimes do our pours late at night so the concrete can set before pressure is again provided in the morning. I can always look to Raymond Knelsen and his crew to provide prompt and efficient service.

Peter's Excavating has given us good service in the track-hoe department. GPEC Engineering always does a superior job in the engineering department. In 10 years of dealing with a host of technical details, I have yet to discover an error of consequence.

The developmental process involves working closely with many individuals and agencies in both the business and government sectors. We must work with engineers, land surveyors, utility companies, land titles officials, planning agencies and not least of all; the local municipality. When such agencies have made their contributions one can start thinking about super-B-train loads of materials; equipment and labourers. Certainly we may never forget the tentacles of the octopus which is our taxation system. This beast with its voracious appetite creates about as much work for me as does any aspect of the operation.

Sometimes when I have spent a month or six weeks away from Rapid View people ask, "What do you do over there?" Simply put, we extend LaCrete's road, watermain, sewer-main, gas, parks, power and lighting systems. At the same time we service the lots with both water and sewer at least to the property line. As well, if a new lot owner catches us before the equipment leaves, we may extend the services onto the lot and maybe even build a driveway. Putting in the water and sewer mains also involves installing fire hydrants and man-holes.

After either a one year or two year warranty period, this whole infrastructure passes into the hands of the Municipal District of MacKenzie #23. It begins charging me taxes on these new lots as of January 1 of the year following construction and registration of the new plan. With that threat hanging over one's head, the developer hopes that his lots will sell quickly.

1997 was our heaviest season to date. Whereas normally we might average 15 lots per season, we, during that year, serviced 38. They constituted Phases 3F and 4A. Relating the events associated with the construction of those two phases alone, would require another book.

The reader might gain some understanding, however, if some of the events of the first weekend of that July were recounted.

We were working on Phase 4A at that time. This involved tying into existing water and sewer mains, cutting through an existing road about four times, locating a gas line several times and trying to avoid chopping off a telephone cable. Preferably at least some of this was to be done after hours so that the large Co-op store complex adjacent could keep functioning. They were concerned about their fresh vegetables which needed to be watered.

To accommodate the Co-op, I left one task, which involved shutting off the water, until about eleven o'clock Saturday night. By the time I had cut the water line and moved a valve, no equipment operator was available to backfill the trench, so it remained open over Sunday. This is not a healthy situation, at best, during days of law-suits and nights of rain.

Sunday night the rains came. The Co-op roof, the nearby roadway, and the diggings pile all directed rain water into our trench with its newly laid but uncovered service pipes.

Water lines aren't so crucial but sewer lines are laid in terms of millimetres. (When we lay sewer mains we use a laser beam and a lath with three marks on it. The top one determines the trench depth. The middle mark indicates the bedding-sand level. The bottom line gives us the top of the pipe.)

By the time I arrived at 6:30 Monday morning, the sewer line we had so carefully laid at a -.04 percent grade was floating on two feet of water. Everything was a muddy, hopeless mess. The rain would not stop and the water continued to flow in.

The engineer arrived shortly after I did, took one look, and walked off without a word. This was totally uncharacteristic for he was normally one of the least tongue-tied people I know even when you eliminate some of his most "florid" superlatives.

So I set to work. The first labourer arrived at nine o'clock. He was gone by the time I got back from ordering gravel with which to re-lay the pipe (I have yet to own my first cell phone). I continued to do the best I could on my own. But I wasn't having any fun at all.

Can you imagine how pleased I was when, having just begun to gain control of the situation, I had the honour of an inspection visit from some of the bright young lads each about 30 years my junior, from the M.D. office? Their judgement seemed to be that maybe the job was not going quite right. Would I shovel some more gravel? No one likes to tax an inferior product, you see.

Some people wonder what has caused me to have such an overwhelming regard for government in general, and tax people in particular. I have come by my opinions honestly and expensively.

The second hired man arrived at 11^{am}. He, at least, stayed to help. After a few hours of track-hoe work, things took on a new complexion, but we were not yet out of the woods.

Even on Tuesday the work was still not going smoothly. By the end of the crew's working day a bottle-neck seemed to exist in whatever direction I turned. That evening I worked by myself until about eleven o'clock. By 3:30 I was again awake so I went back to work as soon as possible. By the time the crew arrived at 7^{am} we were set to progress. My night time efforts paid dividends.

Another of our more sensational evenings also involved muck—truckloads of the stuff. A leak had developed at one of our valves installed during a previous year. I told the people concerned to leave the matter of repairs until I got there with the equipment. The valve was in a particularly tight spot among newly planted lawns, a light post, a drive with a culvert and a survey pin. Hoping to limit the damages, we brought in a wheel hoe with a small bucket. (Our regular track hoe has a five foot bucket.) Jake took about six swipes with his little bucket and realized that there was no hope of gaining on the ooze with his machine. So we thanked him for his efforts and went to work with the track hoe.

The first thing that became apparent was that the lightpole was going to join the slide of ooze. To prevent that unhappy state of affairs we brought over the big crawler tractor and tethered the pole to the blade. Soon the "cat" along with its pole was also volunteering to join the muck slide. In the absence of proper equipment, we tied the light pole to the hoe bucket and gently laid it on the lawn. That was surely the best lit lot in town!

We had long since bid the survey pin adieu. Having eliminated all such indications of civilization, David and later, Peter, the owner of the hoe, could continue mucking. First, they dumped into the adjacent ditch; then they filled the one across the road; and when that was full, the mud flowed onto the lot beyond that ditch. Fortunately that lot belonged to me and there was no one living on it at the time. Finally our pipes started appearing; yet we could not be sure of where they came from or where they were going or if, in fact, they were still going anywhere.

By this time we had quite an audience. I will grant that we were putting on a show that could inspire poets. This was all going on after quitting time. By about nine or ten o'clock I was certainly pleased when Anne-Marie Schlamp very kindly thought to bring supper. (Someone else did that for me on another occasion and I will appreciate those girls for as long as my memory serves me.)

We never did uncover the mainstop valve on the water main. While working from the hoe's bucket, I just pushed a wrench into the mud about fourteen inches to shut the valve off. The curb stop, the second valve, was where the problem was. Someone had failed to make a proper connection. At least that valve was out of the mud where we could repair it.

That done, we began filling the crater, restoring the lawns, repairing the driveway, replanting the street light, raising the culvert and generally try to restore order. We had things looking quite proper and were pleased to have them so. Then we had another of those critical semi-official visits which give me such pleasure.

One of the facts of the developer's life is supervision. First, the engineers design the project; then a second engineering firm is hired by the M.D. at my expense, to check the work of the designing firm. Then the Planning Commission, again at my expense, of course, checks with about eight agencies to see if my plan should be allowed to fly. Soon the surveyors get in on the act. Then I must hire an engineer to oversee the construction process. Next the Municipality checks things out. Then it is back to the Planning Commission and all of this under scrutiny of the M.D. office. Lastly, if one can get past the eagle-eyed Land Titles people, he has a registered document. To put the icing on the cake, Paul Martin then goes on television and compliments himself for having done so well with the budget.

When the construction process is almost complete we do several tests. First we flush the sewer line; then we put in a large ball while running some water through. If it comes out at the next manhole we know that no one left a stray shoe in the pipe.

The water-main must undergo a pressure test. The new lines have to be isolated and pressurized to about two to three times normal pressure. The pressure must stay almost constant for two hours after which the system is again pressurized to the exact same reading, and the amount of water required to restore pressure is measured. A formula involving the number of unions in the system tells the engineer whether the project passes. If it does not, you plan to start digging to find the problem—if you can tell where.

One summer I blew the system apart twice before I realized that my gauge wasn't working. The first time I pressured up, the gauge went to 62 pounds before the needle suddenly dropped. Things had blown apart. After repairing the damages, we poured even more concrete and backfilled quite extensively to keep the plug, and all else, in place. When even that blew apart at the identical 62 pound reading, I decided to throw away the gauge (which had been new the previous summer). Sure enough, at the third try, when we used a new gauge, there was no problem.

Those high pressure washer pumps generate a lot of pressure when they have a six inch main to work with. (pi x r x r x pressure/sq. in. Remember?).

By now the reader may have the impression that things always go wrong. They don't. Usually our work goes very well, but one is inclined to remember the "extracurricular events".

There are many pluses in the equation. Once we get away from any existing infrastructure, the digging conditions are invariably excellent. After continuous summers of digging, we came across our first rock in 1997. Too bad we hadn't dug it out as a memorial.

The soil is likely best described as sandy loam. Left undisturbed it remains firm and solid, but once it is moved, it handles somewhat as sand. Stickiness during rains is not really a problem. We have never had a cave-in as we worked in previously undisturbed soil. Cave-ins are one of the very real threats in that type of work.

After cave-ins, one of the most serious hazards is a gas line. We became so used to digging in previously untouched areas, that I'm afraid we forgot that things could be quite different from our norm.

During one coffee break one of the labourers and the hoe operator were at Kay's Café discussing the job when the thought came to them that there was likely a gas line in the area being dug. They were absolutely correct. (Please be aware that they were digging with a no-nonsense track machine with a great boom and its five-foot bucket to match.)

If they had taken even one more swipe, that 3" high pressure gas line would have roared into a volcano, possibly a fiery one. The people who advise us to, "Call before you dig," are not just "whistling Dixie".

Rumour has it that one contractor went broke after a piece of his equipment cut a fibre-optic line between Calgary and Edmonton.

Yes, there have been a few rough spots in the trail, but a person should not expect to have things otherwise. Thus, because "hope springs eternal in the human breast," I am looking forward to building the 18 lots on 105th Avenue. Then, when all has gone well—or almost—Vangard will be able to accommodate some of the 40 LaCrete couples who will likely marry this summer. As I write this in March, 1998, people are already inquiring regarding our next project(s).

On Henry and Luella's 40th anniversary

Rear (left–right): Lanna-Marie, Luella, Henry, Laurella (husband Brett away) Ann & Arlyn

Front (left–right): Lyndell (holding Lorenzo), Daniella (holding Lezlie), Kiern & BrynnJoyce

Chapter 28

The Rapid View Chapter

Although Luella never complained, living life far from childhood friends and relatives was not without its pensive moments. Hardly ever did she have an opportunity to experience a musical concert or attend a family function. We always had good friends near at hand but the home-home was a weekend visit precluding 15 hours away. Since Luella had been good enough to follow me around for 35 years, I thought it only proper that I respect her wishes in retirement.

Several years before we planned to move, we began looking around in the Rapid View area for a suitable place. We liked the idea of moving to this community because one of the churches Luella's father oversaw during his years as bishop is located here. As we looked about, someone suggested that the Brown place might be coming up for sale. This holding of 11 acres suited us well. It was the fine growth of spruce all around the yard that appealed to Luella. Browns were sorry to leave this, their home of 50 years, but for reasons of health plus some charity, they agreed to sell it to us. We were not yet quite ready to move when the Browns felt they had to go, so Albert Esau kept the fire stoked until we could move in.

What is it like to be retired? Do you miss teaching? What do you do? Are some of the questions that people ask us. Retirement isn't the drag that I thought it might be. Actually I quite enjoy my freedom and sometimes wonder how I found time to go to school every day .

As for missing teaching, I could still happily teach Junior High math and such subjects, but I cannot say that I miss having to go to school every day. There are too many other activities to keep me occupied. In any event, it was never my way to pine for that which is not.

What do I do? Mostly what is at the top of the list at the moment. Usually that which is in that spot and at the top of the pile of paper that seems always to be on my desk is something to do with Vangard Realty. Vangard is the real bread winner in this family so we must give him his proper place. This is not a full time job, but there is a multiplicity of duties to attend to when a person is involved with every aspect of the operation. The actual construction aspect takes less than a month per year. The accounting and planning are ongoing all year long.

Some of our time goes into the various activities of the church. As a deacon, I go to council meetings. Sometimes I participate in special numbers. I take my turn teaching the adult Sunday School class. A few weeks ago we spent a day hauling firewood for our outside boiler. Yesterday a work bee built 32 bunks for Bethel Gospel Camp. Last summer I spent some days at camp nailing siding to some camp buildings.

Sometimes I help my neighbours with this or that including, most often, work with cattle or helping with the harvest.

Before the last election, I worked for my buddy, Preston Manning, and some of the kindred spirits in his cause.

Cattle seemed like an interesting sideline, especially since this is cattle country. Salers were in the news when that particular urge hit me. Since I had limited acres I thought I should go for quality and raise purebred bulls to sell. But my bulls couldn't understand why they should stay home when the boss got to go on extended leaves. Furthermore, looking after the herd was too time consuming so my neighbour is keeping the herd on a calf-share basis.

Even though maintenance requirements have diminished considerably since the departure of the bulls whose joy in life was to destroy things, there remains much to be done in that department. Lyndell did a lot of work in the interior of the house. Arlyn helped me side it. Arlyn and Brett helped me build fences and corrals. Last summer I covered the large pig barn roof with metal.

Since I needed hay, I rented 60 acres from my neighbour. These I broke, picked tons of rock off, and seeded to oats and then hay. We also bought a bush quarter which I am taming by increments. I've had about 40 acres cleared of willows.

One of my current enthusiasms involves the team of Norwegian Fiords that I bought last fall. The mare was semi-broke, but the colt had only been trained to lead. I had never trained a young horse before, so this has been an interesting, if time consuming, experience. I will not even begin to relate the details of the process other than to say that he wants to make a great issue of every detail. And just because he accepted scratching on the left side, was not to say that it was okay to scratch the right side. That little hurdle had to be addressed separately. Genne Nolan has helped me with the driving. We have driven them four or five times. I believe I can handle them by myself now, especially now that our education has included the matter of school buses. All of the foregoing activities are not that big a deal. They are things farmers do. The matter of the Internet, however, is major.

Lyndell and Daniela are with Campus Crusade for Christ. Their purpose is to engage in interactive evangelism world wide on the Internet. The project has only just begun to roll, but during a recent campaign in the lower mainland of B.C. 14,000 people visited their site for an average of just under eight minutes each. People from such countries as India, Thailand, Indonesia, and Tanzania, Egypt, and many others are showing interest. I wish to contribute time and effort to this major initiative. Never

Author Henry Enns trades his wings for four-wheeled travel with grandchildren

has the Christian Church had such an opportunity to spread the only message that really counts. I have rarely felt as compelled and urgent about anything as I do about this project. Part of the reason for this feeling of urgency is that I believe that the Lord's return is very near and once that happens it will be "curtains" for most, if not all, such activities.

One of the events of note that has transpired since we arrived on this scene was our fortieth wedding anniversary. My three brothers and one sister, most of our children, all of our grandchildren, as well as other relatives and friends were able to be with us. We appreciated their presence and good will. Living at the centre of things, as we do, it is good to receive that sort of visit. Now I am looking forward to a visit from the grandchildren.

I wish to draw this chronicle to a close on a personal note. One of the most pleasant experiences of contentment I have come to appreciate occurs on a Saturday night. The day has been busy; worthwhile things have been accomplished; I have had a nice warm bath; Luella has provided clean and fresh bedding; I'm tired and ready for a good sleep. My prayer is brief, (of necessity for the time is brief). "Thank you, Jesus!"

I think that Saturday experience is a microcosm of my life in general. Although I'm in no great rush to begin eternity—there will be lots left even if its onset is postponed for a period—the thought of the transition is nevertheless rather pleasant. Life has been an interesting experience, but it must end. Worthwhile things have been accomplished; the dirt has been washed away; a good rest seems justified. "Thank you, Jesus!"

Appendix A
Northland School Division

During the period of growth and transition at Little Buffalo, Northland School Division came into being; and over a period of time assumed full responsibility for what evolved. Its beginnings should be considered.

As the boarding school concept faded during the 1950's and 1960's, many communities, like Little Buffalo, needed schools. These settlements were scattered over a vast region of Northern Alberta. They were often remote and isolated, their needs seen to be different. Existing school jurisdictions like the Fort Vermilion, Peace River, High Prairie and Slave Lake School Divisions were considered as being ill equipped to meet the needs of the Native communities. It was decided that a new and differing educational entity was required. Northland School Division was envisaged as being the answer.

Northland, as it is usually called, was born in February 1961. Its mandate was to provide schooling in remote areas. Invariably the communities served were closer to an existing school jurisdiction than they were to Northland's office in Edmonton, but the fact that the students were Native somehow seemed to justify this inconvenience.

In time Northland's office was moved to Peace River. This move brought some improvement in communications. Having maintenance people in Peace River rather than in Edmonton meant they might have to drive only six hours instead of ten in order to discover that the school was cold because the fuel had run out.

The concept of a distinct school division has its points, but in my estimation this idea of a separate school system for a particular people is a mistake. The idea is part of the distinct-society concept which is also a fundamental error. How can Canada be expected to function as a unit when its population is fragmented into its various people groups? "Divide and conquer" has long been a recipe for defeat. Why does our nation allow itself to be weakened by disunity? Who is seeking to conquer us? Could it be our Federal Government?

If people living in our distinct-people groups were specimens from Mars, some case might be made for isolationism but they aren't from Mars or any place close to it. They are people much like myself. When I consider how easily our white children blended in with the other children, and when I consider how readily the Little Buffalo children learned, how skilful they were, how gifted, clean, and self-respecting, I am further dismayed by the chasms artificially created among us.

Are sub-groups perhaps created so jobs might result? Do we need an Indian Affairs so that we can have a large Indian Affairs bureaucracy? I certainly do not see where the Indians need such a department and if they don't, exactly who does? Why not replace it with a Department of Ukranian Affairs? I'll bet it would do a lot less damage! When you stop to think about it, many people would lose their jobs if society functioned well. Lawyers need criminals; social workers need hapless children and broken families; Government needs dependants. If all the sheep are in one pasture, one shepherd can tend them. If they are in ten pastures, ten shepherds find employment. What a dreadful, heartless, selfish way of using unsuspecting people! All this time many are caused to believe they are being helped. How disappointed they will be when they discover they were merely being used. Even as I edit this manuscript in early 1999, Russians are freezing and starving. Is it because their land lacks the resources to sustain them? Certainly not! They are the victims of a rotten system, but unfortunately, even though the system is largely discredited and defunct its legacy persists.

Appendix B

Northern Geography

When one observes the drainage patterns of Alberta, an interesting pattern emerges. A figure somewhat resembling the pattern of the veins in a net-veined leaf becomes apparent. In a leaf there are the lesser veins joined to greater veins, connected to the stem of the leaf. The leaf in its turn is fastened to a twig which joins a branch growing out of the trunk. The flow of water is in reverse to the flow in a drainage basin, but the resemblance is interesting even if opposite.

Ultimately the northern two thirds of Alberta, plus a vast portion of the North West Territories, is drained by one river system, the tremendous MacKenzie.

Where only northern Alberta is taken into account, three main river systems are required to do the task; the Hay River, the Peace, and the Athabasca. The Hay flows directly into Great Slave Lake. The Peace and the Athabasca join forces to become the Slave before their waters flow into Great Slave Lake. In due course the Slave, together with a host of lesser rivers, become the MacKenzie which is the vehicle to transport the water to the Arctic Ocean.

Before the days of the airplane and the road these drainage patterns determined not only the flow of water but also the flow of human traffic. For explorer MacKenzie the incentives to range far and wide were curiosity and a desire to learn. The information gleaned was of great value to the fur industry in which the waterways were crucial. For most explorers and travellers the impetus to journey on their routes took the shape of an "S" with two vertical lines through it.

The MacKenzie drainage basin was immensely rich in furs. For example, the great delta in what is now Wood Buffalo Park succoured the largest muskrats to be found about anywhere on earth.

The reason for the existence of the vast delta was the flooding which sometimes occurred before the advent of the Bennett Dam in British Columbia. When the run-off of the Peace could not be accommodated by the Slave, due to ice jams or whatever, the flow of one or more of the four rivers which join Lake Athabasca and the main Slave River would be reversed for a time. When the crest subsided, the waters flowed north again. By that time the delta, acting as a great sponge, was soaked and able to sustain tremendous wildlife.

Because this flooding is of such huge benefit to this area, the Natives can't always quite understand why floods elsewhere are regarded as such tragedies.

One downside to the flooding, however, concerns the huge herds of Buffalo which make Wood Buffalo Park their home. Sometimes some of them do get caught by flood waters, causing drowning. Even so their numbers offer a sight to behold from the air.

Interestingly, the two Alberta towns which vie for "oldest town in Alberta" status are both found in this area. The dispute is difficult to settle because if Fort Chipewyan's original situation on the south side of Lake Athabasca is considered, it takes the honour. If Fort Chipewyan's present relocated situation is taken to be the place of its origin, then Fort Vermilion must be accorded the distinction.

Both towns figure prominently in early Alberta history because both were on important water routes. Fort Vermilion was accessed by the Upper Peace, while Fort Chipewyan was served by the Athabasca water system. The place of demarcation was at The Chutes some 40 miles down river from Fort Vermilion.

The Chutes are really a small water fall. There was no time when this obstacle could be conquered by river traffic. Other rapids further down river on the Peace could be navigated during high water.

In the early days skilled river pilots knew where to find the channels. They were assisted by some navigational aides. Today no such help is available. Thus, The Chutes marked journey's end for both up river and down river traffic. If there was to be any movement of freight past the chutes it was done with wagons.

Near this parting of the ways the Hudson's Bay Company established a post. The remains of this post may yet be seen at the confluence of the Little Red and Peace Rivers.

Today the Mackenzie Highway and all its tributaries serve the many Alberta communities of that general area as well as much of the Northwest Territories. The presence of this road network plus air traffic have rendered the river steamer obsolete.

This is not yet the case where the Athabasca River system is concerned. Where humans once toiled to move the freight boats, today powerful tugs tow strings of up to six barges bringing freight to such communities as Fort Chipewyan on Lake Athabasca.

Part of the reason for the continuing river traffic along the Athabasca is the difficult terrain. The tremendous Athabasca Delta would surely daunt the most imaginative road engineer as well as any funding agency. Furthermore, the thin population hardly justifies the huge outlay which would be required.

As things stand, any would-be traveller by road into Fort Chipewyan or Fort Smith by that eastern route will find himself waiting in Fort McMurray for freeze-up. A good paved road would take him as far as the tar sands projects, but beyond that it's a winter road over much ice.

Even the winter road is a real problem as I write during this February of 1998, the winter of El Niño. Though temperatures in the Fort Chipewyan region have been quite normal, the ice bridges don't hold. The warm waters coming in from the south erode the ice. The consequence is that heavy trucks which normally bring in such freight as propane are unable to haul. Had the people been allowed to use that fine fire-killed wood in Wood Buffalo Park they wouldn't have become so dependent on the White Man's propane. Now he can't provide it and there is a problem. But the Park was off limits. We revisionists must tamper.

Mind you, the stranded traveller, if of a mechanical bent, might find himself well entertained at the tar sands. The equipment used there is truly awe inspiring. The shovels dwarf everything that comes near. Monster trucks haul 360 tons. Interestingly, one of the preferred drivers for these new trucks is a female former member of the mine's secretarial staff.

The vital statistics employed exhaust our superlatives. Someone has surely written a book on that subject.

Although Alberta is only indirectly affected, transportation along the MacKenzie River should be mentioned.

Hay River on the west end of Great Slave Lake is the largest fresh water harbour in Canada. That harbour is the southern terminus for the barge and other traffic which operates on the Lake and north along the MacKenzie River. This is a significant freight route but the traffic run by the Canadian Coast Guard out of Hay River is also important.

The MacKenzie River, like its namesake highway, is a crucial link joining supply centres like Edmonton to the communities of the North.

But rivers like the MacKenzie and the Peace can also be significant barriers. Several bridges of the conventional type span the Peace. No one has yet tried to bridge the MacKenzie. A logical explanation for this reticence must be that it more nearly resembles a lake than a river in some places.

One of the real pluses of northern winters is that ice-bridges can be built. They are a real boon. They make possible all manner of activity which cannot happen in summer. For example, frozen rivers and muskegs enable the logging industry to spring into life, even if for only about three frantic months. Likewise, winter is the time for most seismic and drilling activity.

In the absence of bridges of either the temporary or permanent variety, ferries are used at several locations. Two significant ferries cross the Peace at Tompkins Landing, and the MacKenzie beyond Hay River. During freeze-up or break-up no one crosses at Tompkins Landing, but some provision is made for crossing the Mackenzie River for the benefit of Yellowknife, especially. Helicopters are employed at that crossing taking both lighter vehicles and passengers.

At one juncture Alberta Transportation tried to use a hovercraft at Tompkins but that effort proved to be an expensive disaster. The hovercraft was to hover over both ice and water or variations thereof. As it hovered it was to propel itself along cables which would also serve to direct it.

When the much awaited launching was to transpire, crowds gathered. Unfortunately, the new craft was so slow that the former ferry was pressed back into action. Not only was the new ferry slow, but no one seems to have thought of the fact that when that ice began moving it was going to take any cable with it. Additionally, this hovering ferry had the annoying habit of spattering profusely over vehicles freshly laundered for that anticipated trip. Before long someone in B.C. bought himself a hovercraft—cheap.

Now a double-hulled ferry with a no-nonsense propulsion system takes the largest vehicles across the Peace in a matter of minutes.

I wouldn't leave my reader with the impression that ice bridges are not without their challenges.

Appendix C

Land Clearing and Scarification

Modern equipment is massive and effective. Relatively little sweat of the brow is required—just much fruit of the wallet.

If a homestead applicant happens to be fortunate enough to go through the selection process successfully, he is free to proceed with clearing and breaking.

The first machine required is a brush cutter. This machine looks somewhat like a huge V-shaped snowplow. There is one major difference. Built at right angles to the bottom of the vertical pushing surfaces is a sharpened blade about a foot wide. As the crawler tractor on which all this is mounted pushes relentlessly forward, the trees are shorn off just above the ground and pushed to both sides allowing for the passage of the machine. Even the largest of the trees must give way when a D8 is used.

When the bush is lying, the next machine required is the piler. This again is a massive machine which reminds one of a bulldozer blade but it is both wider and higher. It also has foot-long teeth along the lower edge. With this accessory the crawler can windrow cut trees. Trees which covered vast areas can be pushed into field-length piles so that they can be burned.

Much of the brush thus eliminated is worthless. Timber suitable for sawing is salvaged before the brush cutter is sent in. In recent years, scientists have discovered uses for the lowly poplar, so it is salvaged. Poplar is of little use for lumber but can be profitably used for chipboard or paper.

When the trees are out of the way the area is ready for breaking. Special breaking plows are used. Some have four shares and might be 30 or 40 feet long. These plows roll over the ground, turning up and tearing apart the stumps and roots.

Root-picking is the next procedure. This used to be a very tedious task, when done by hand. Now it is just a matter of machines and dollars. Sometimes the field is first harrowed with large, flexible, chain-like harrows to bring up the wood, but often the big root picker goes on right after the plow. Usually the root picker consists of a large pipe, maybe 36" in diameter, mounted on a frame with three wheels. Welded to this drum in a spiral formation are about three rows of teeth. The teeth are somewhat wedge-shaped pieces of flat-iron about 10" long. As the machine is pulled forward the drum is rotated, either by the power take-off or a hydraulic pump. This rotation is in the direction opposite to the revolution of the wheels. The resulting action kicks the roots forward and into windrows which are moved across the field as this operation progresses.

These windrows of roots are then burned.

Now the cultivation process can begin. Usually a deep-tillage cultivator is used in the next pass to bring up more roots. Likely the field will then be re-picked.

The end is in sight. By then some young farmer has developed a gleam in his eye!

Closely akin to this procedure is the scarification process carried on in the forested areas. The objective in this process, however, is the growing of trees. In this procedure a huge plow is pulled through a logged area tearing up soil, moss, stumps—everything. Tree planters then place their seedlings.

A more recent procedure involves a track-hoe which works through low areas building mounds on which trees are planted. The purpose of the mounds is to keep the trees out of the water.

Appendix D

The LaCrete Business Community

As the community of LaCrete progresses the business sector keeps pace. Vangard is happy to be part of the picture both as a recipient of services and as a contributor.

Of the businesses, Vangard is most reliant on Knelsen's, whose concrete business has been supplemented and complemented by the sand and gravel business. One evening last summer the rains held off long enough for us to get in a little road work. Knelsens delivered about 460 yards of gravel in three hours and they didn't even work up a sweat. I suspect if their whole fleet had been operative they could have hauled the lot in one trip. The good services their company give are worth a great deal to me as I do my projects. Not many company owners would be prepared to deliver a yard of concrete at eleven o'clock at night so I could pour a valve into place.

Another business, the destiny of which has never been in doubt, is LaCrete Tire and Battery whose chief concern seems to be that things keep rolling. Nor did they stop with tires; they also do mechanical work. Does anyone need a snow-machine, power saw or lawn mower? Go see the lads at Tuffline. They'll happily sell you one of each.

From my observations, implement dealerships come and go but in the instance of John Deere, I believe Frontier Power has come to stay.

Because the list goes on, the needs of the local farming and industrial community are well met. Though Edmonton, the principal supply centre, is 500 road miles south transportation is not a major problem. Several trucking firms like LaCrete Transport and Schmidt's Trucking Service handle the task. Usually a telephone call followed by an all night run puts one day delivery within reach.

Wiebe's Transport and a host of other lesser operations attend to the bulk hauling of grain, lumber, fertilizer and salt. Even exports to the Japanese lumber markets can be readily looked after. My guess is that LaCrete has more Kenworths per capita than any place on earth.

While one of the principal employers in the community is LaCrete Sawmills, which specializes in dimensions demanded by the Japanese market, the principal player in the forestry sector is the big Diashawa mill at High Level. Only a few people commute from LaCrete to actually work at the mill. The principal benefit to LaCrete is in the bush work. Most of that work is attended to by LaCrete based companies.

Many local trucks and truckers serve in the forestry sectors supplying chip and log hauling services to sawmills, and pulp and paper mills in such centres as Slave Lake, Peace River,

Grande Prairie and Manning. The families tend to remain in LaCrete.

People wonder how it is that I and other developers can develop and sell lots year after year when most small towns struggle to exist. Recently, a sign on the outskirts of a hamlet was seen to read, "Lots for Sale, $300.00 with 10% down payment." We do not post that type of sign at LaCrete.

First, I explain I'm not the only show in town. In fact, when we did Phase 2D, Vangard serviced an additional 11 lots across the street for another developer. In the 1995–96 seasons these other developers provided about 70 residential lots. The commercial area is developing nicely as well.

Part of the answer to the question about opportunities to sell lots is found as one considers the nature of this dynamic community. The town's vitality builds on itself. There are several considerations that enter the explanation. An understanding of the growth phenomenon requires an understanding of the community which the reader may have gained through a reading of chapters 19 and 22.

Furthermore, it is important to recognize that LaCrete is a religious community, "religion" being read in the broad sense of the word. This fact influences much of life in this community. This characteristic has a cohesive effect because the religious mindset influences how people feel about the family.

Large families were and still are the appreciated norm. When large families mature they need many homes. The sense of family, kinship and community is very real. Visiting around is the foremost local pastime. Thus, if at all possible, people want to remain in their community. This holds for seniors as well as young people. If young people or a family must, they may leave to work outside, but when an opportunity appears, back they move.

Occasionally there is a minor exodus but the impact on the local population seems negligible. The destination of choice is usually Bolivia. People move there for religious reasons. Increasing secularization is a definite reality at LaCrete, but the trend is apparent in Bolivia too. The result is an amazing amount of commuting as people search for the best setting for their families.

Other considerations that impact on the real estate scene involve the physical realities of northern Alberta. For instance, LaCrete is primarily a prosperous agricultural area inhabited by people with farming in their blood. Even today the desire to farm is accommodated through homestead-type expansion. Some homestead land is still made available periodically through a draw system. One of the consequences of this reality is that, as farming areas go, LaCrete is quite densely populated.

Two other major factors contributing to the population base, and therefore to the need for lots, are the forest and oil industries. Good money is usually available at Rainbow Lake and Zama City—two important oil producing areas three hours to the northwest. Even though money is to be made in these areas, they are not regarded as suitable places for homes for growing children. Thus the pattern of life is often to go out, earn some money to make a start, and go back home—where we then may need a lot.

The most significant factor in the equation, next to farming, is the forest industry. LaCrete Sawmills employs some 150 people. The mill in High Level is a much larger operation. As well, there are about eight lesser mills in the LaCrete area. The larger mills are provided with logs by 5 major contractors who are all headquartered at LaCrete. That is where they have their large service shops, and where the extensive inventories of equipment are stored and restored through the summer. LaCrete is where the workforce resides. True, most of the people employed in the forest industries prefer to live in the rural areas, but a significant number needs lots.

Appendix E

Little Buffalo Co-op Starts to Pay Off

This story, written by Stephen Cook, appeared in the September 13, 1972 Record/Gazette and is reprinted here with permission.

The journey to the out of the way community of Little Buffalo is hard on a vehicle. If you've been on a back road in Africa or the Caribbean then you have an idea of what it's like.

Once you're past the Three Creeks Ranger Station you leave the gravel road and hit a narrow dirt track, with heavy brush on either side. At the very end of this track, some 46 miles later, is Little Buffalo, and I might add a lot of enthusiastic people.

And they have every reason to be. An industry has been brought right to their front door.

But getting the co-op to the area was no easy matter and it took the community's only white man five years of persuading different government departments to make the first move.

Henry Enns, a quiet man by common standards, and the principal of the local school that teaches children up to grade 8, has lived in Little Buffalo for 12 years with his wife and children.

Gently pushing his glasses back onto the bridge of his nose, Henry related how most of the community (there are 20 families, roughly 150 people) relied heavily on trapping as a means of making a living.

"Yet the times had changed and it was time the people were introduced to a more stable livelihood," he continued.

"So I started writing letters to the government asking for land on their behalf, and financial assistance." Trapping, explained Henry, was the type of occupation that demanded a person work hard for a short period of time during the year and the rest of the time was your own.

But in Henry's opinion it wasn't helping the Indians to better themselves, hence he fought for a grant that would be used to establish a co-op, with the result a co-op would give Indians seasonal work but of a different and more permanent nature.

Objections from government departments came strong and furious.

The Department of Forestry didn't go for Henry's project saying it would harm the environment.

ARDA, a department responsible for developing land gave sympathetic hearings to Henry's letters but turned a deaf ear to his initial request.

This department was eventually renamed the Human Resources Development Authority, and through this body the final go ahead was given.

Apparently ARDA focused the government's attention on the

fact that the land being asked for was crown land and that it had not been surveyed.

"They finally said there was no point in us getting a grant without the proper land," grinned Henry, "when I look back that wasn't such a bad argument."

All this took five years to say, but finally the government saw light of day and in May 1970, the Little Buffalo Farming Co-op was officially registered with the government. A six man board consisted of local men, and their job is to oversee the management of the farm, of which Henry is the secretary-treasurer.

The government handed over five sections of land and a promise that over a four-year period the co-op would receive a $189,000 grant.

The community's first job was to clear the land and prepare it for cattle and crops, and later they went ahead and bought 20 head of cattle. To date that figure stands at 100, and it's hoped by next spring the co-op will be able to start selling their young steer calves.

Manager of the co-op is Fleuri L'Hirondelle, a Metis, born eight miles away from Little Buffalo. He also runs a farm of his own.

"We want to get into the cattle business in a big way," he said as he stepped down from his tractor to talk. "The winter's hard on them at first, but they get used to it eventually."

So far the co-op has spent $25,000 on machinery and $17,000 on preparing the land.

On the subject of money, labourers working for the organization receive officially $1.90 an hour; however, they only receive about two-thirds of that amount.

The remainder is put aside to support the co-op's capital expenditures.

Although, as Henry pointed out, the men themselves wanted money saved out of their wages, it does at times create bad feeling. Still they do have a comforting thought as they now have $9,000 in a trust fund for the future development of the farm.

The co-op grows oats and barley and the board is looking forward to an exceptionally good harvest later this month. Last year the farm yielded a crop from 200 acres; this year it will come from 300. In 1971 the co-op collected 1,000 bushels of oats and barley, 200 loads of silage and 6,000 bushels of grass.

It's possibly because of the band's relative success at the co-op that they have received some requests from people wishing to move into the area.

"We try to discourage white people from coming in and buying up land," said Henry. In some ways it's the isolation of this place that tends to protect the Indian from overzealous white men.

In conversation Mr. L'Hirondelle talked cautiously about the Indian's progress on the co-op and how they were adjusting to it.

"A lot of them don't understand; I guess about half of them fully appreciate what's going on," he said slowly.

Scratching his head he went on, "It's hard for Indians to change their way, from trapping to farming. The boys work pretty fair now that things are moving fast and there's lots of work available."

Mildred Mallinger who works along side Henry at the school,

Henry Enns (left) and Fleuri L'Hirondelle
at the Little Buffalo Co-op in 1972

and incidentally started up the school 19 years ago, says the Indian does have a long way to go but, she adds, they have improved greatly over the years.

"What the white man has done is come along and yank the Indian out of the stone age over a limited number of years and it's just not long enough for him to adjust to their lifestyle overnight," she said.

Where there's people there has got to be housing and that's a sore point with Henry.

"Some government people came out from the Alberta Housing Corporation three months ago and we haven't heard from them since," he said calmly.

For the future, two of the five sections of land are to be broken into eight quarters and shared among people working for the co-op.

"Already there are eight people who have tentatively spoken for a quarter of land, yet the offer is open to all," said Henry.

The community's only commercial enterprise is a small store run by the L'Hirondelle family. Their nearest competition is at Cadotte Lake a few miles down the road. There is a church, which Henry conducts service in as they don't have a resident minister.

There is also a stud mill. It was built in March of last year and cost the co-op about $2,250. The system at the moment is that an Indian collects his wood, brings it to the mill and as payment for having it shaved and cut, he deposits about a third of it.

"Business has been fairly slow, but we are hoping it will pick up this fall," explained Henry.

As I packed my truck to leave I sensed for some unknown reason I was in a desperate hurry to get out of the enclosed area and speed down an open highway. The people were friendly enough, even though they were supersensitive to my presence.

But then that type of surrounding is unnatural to me and not to them.

There is no doubt in my mind the revolutionary step taken by the government, even though they used taxpayers' money to do it, was probably the best thing ever done to help the Indian in Alberta.